REVOLUTION
FOR DUMMIES

REVOLUTION FOR DUMMIES

LAUGHING THROUGH THE ARAB SPRING

BASSEM YOUSSEF

DEY ST.
An Imprint of WILLIAM MORROW

DEY ST.

HarperCollins books may be purchased for educational, business, or sales promotional use. For information, please email the Special Markets Department at SPsales@harpercollins.com.

A hardcover edition of this book was published in 2017 by Dey Street Books, an imprint of William Morrow.

FIRST DEY STREET BOOKS PAPERBACK EDITION PUBLISHED 2017.

Designed by Renata De Oliveira

Library of Congress Cataloging-in-Publication Data has been applied for.

ISBN 978-0-06-244690-9

17 18 19 20 21   LSC   10 9 8 7 6 5 4 3 2 1

TO MY DAUGHTER, NADIA—YOU ARE A VERY HARD ACT TO FOLLOW. MY UNBORN CHILDREN WILL HAVE TO COME UP WITH UNTHINKABLE FEATS JUST TO MATCH YOUR LEVEL OF AWESOMENESS.

TO MY WIFE—I KNOW YOU DIDN'T EXPECT THIS KIND OF MARRIAGE OR LIFE, BUT HEY . . . NOT A DULL MOMENT, BABE. WITHOUT YOUR PATIENCE, RESILIENCE, AND SUPPORT I WOULDN'T HAVE AMOUNTED TO ANYTHING.

TO MY OLDER BROTHER AND MY FRIEND, TAMER YOUSSEF—YOU ARE ALL THAT IS LEFT AFTER OUR PARENTS DEPARTED THIS WORLD. YOU ARE ALL THAT REMAINS OF AN EGYPT I ONCE KNEW.

CONTENTS

PART TWO: RISKY BUSINESS

PART THREE: THE CLOWN, THE TRAITOR, THE OUTCAST

AUTHOR'S NOTE
(or Why Did I Buy This Book Again?)

You might expect me to narrate the epic events of the Arab Spring—to tell you the details of the geopolitical and sociological circumstances (whatever that means) that led to the various Arab revolutions throughout the Middle East, and the great hopes and aspirations that came with them. You might expect me to give you an in-depth analysis of how everything there now seems to be a total desperate mess. But do you really care about that? Be honest, don't you just want to make it *seem* like you understand the Middle East by dropping knowledge bombs (at least these don't hurt) on your friends, but you'd rather hear it from that Egyptian guy you saw a couple of times on *The Daily Show*? I mean, even people from my country stopped caring a long time ago about *why* we are a shitshow. For us in the Middle East, injustice, oppression, and the insanity of justifying them are now just an integral part of our government-sponsored daily news; nothing surprises us anymore. We have somehow embraced the failure, disappointment, and futility of what everything has become, the same way you guys embrace PBS: you don't know why it's still on the air, but somehow you've all accepted it.

Plus, if you really wanted to get an objective, in-depth study about what the hell is happening in the Middle East, you'd go get a book published by some wonky think tank in Washington. There are dozens of these books claiming they've got the "answer" for what the hell is happening there . . . yet the Middle East is still a big mess. So either no one is reading these books or even heavily funded policy institutions don't know jack shit about us. So let me give you some advice. If you think you are ever going to truly understand what is happening in the Middle East . . . *stop!*

Instead of giving you some underwhelming history lesson, I'm going to tell you my story—what happened to me while the revolution occurred and my unexpected role within it. Yeah, sure, "my story" makes me sound important, but really it is just a ploy to keep you interested! Hell, you might think I'm an arrogant son of a bitch for thinking that people would buy a book just to hear "my story," and you are right; who the fuck do I think I am? But then again, you're the same country that published and bought biographies about Paris Hilton and Heidi Montag. Hell, even Fabio wrote a fucking book. So if you're looking to read about fake boobs, sex tapes, or a man with long blond hair who half-nakedly rides a horse—then you're right—you won't care about my story.

But the problem is I have already received an advance from the publisher (which I've already spent), so either I come up with a book or hustle my way through paying back the advance. And since I can't really escape the publisher by fleeing back to my country, from which I had to escape more than two years ago (more on that later!), I might as well write the goddamn book.

How my story is not already in development to be an awards-season darling is beyond me. Picture this: an Arab man (played by Javier Bardem with an accent because, you know, Hollywood's diversity problem) grows up to save a *few lives* as a heart surgeon, but when a whole region experiences the biggest clusterfuck in its history, he saves the *whole nation* with his jokes. The writers may have to take some liberties in order to write a happy ending and appeal to an American audience, but enjoy your second Oscar, Javier.

However, the movie has yet to be made, so you're just going to have to read this book. Through it you will see how ignorance, xenophobia, racism, and everything that Donald Trump stands for can transcend borders, cultures, and religions. You will find how easy it is to brainwash masses of people, however well informed they think they are, without the funding of Fox News, the pure hatred that is Ann Coulter, or the Bible. After the fame and the short-lived celebrity life I had in Egypt, my story is all I have left. So consider me your companion for the next seventy thousand words (yes, that's the minimum the publisher asked for). If you're lucky, reading this book may incite an interesting conversation (or fight!) at a bar. In certain parts of the country, I bet you'll look and sound exotic (i.e., "un-American") reading a short history of the Arab Spring through the eyes of the "Jon Stewart of Egypt." If you are liberal, you will attract other liberals—you know, being inter- ested in the matters of the world and shit. If you're really lucky, you might even get laid tonight by some hot chick! (If you are a woman, that last sentence is totally sexist and was planted there by my editor.) And if you are a Republican, well . . . I'm sorry! That must be really tough for you.

Most books about the Arab Spring start on January 25, 2011, when the Egyptian Revolution officially began. It's the logical jumping-off point, and trust me, we will get there. But remember, this book is also about me, and I'm the one writing it . . . so let's jump forward a couple of years and start with something to really grab you, like the time I was trying to flee from my own country, to become an ex–funny man, a fugitive on the run.

REVOLUTION
FOR DUMMIES

A HEART SURGEON BREAKING BAD

EXODUS ON EMIRATES AIRLINES

NOVEMBER 11, 2014

Cairo doesn't have any traffic lights. Well, it really does, but the streets are regulated by the sheer volume of vehicles chugging through its lanes, all trying to get somewhere while getting nowhere. This is how you know you are in an Arab country: you are either stuck in a revolution or in traffic. Egypt has the distinction of having both.

On November 11, stalled in that same notorious traffic, I was dead silent. I kept refreshing my Twitter feed, noting that the news of the verdict against me had yet to break.

Abbas, my friend who was accompanying me, asked if I was doing okay. I mumbled that I was fine.

As the chaos of the streets reeled around me, I looked outside the window and saw an old billboard with my face on it. Not many months ago this face was on almost every billboard in every main street in Cairo—the face of the most popular show in Egypt and the Arab world.

Tarek, my friend in Dubai, kept calling Abbas's phone to get updates on our status.

"We haven't arrived at the airport yet," Abbas answered. "Yes, Emirates airlines' flight is on time. Will tell you when we pass the customs check."

Tarek had escaped Egypt a year before me. Never did I think I would be following in his footsteps and running from the same country that voted me the "most popular media personality" three years in a row. What's a popularity contest worth if it doesn't offer immunity from political exile?

"Do you think they'll let me travel?" I asked Abbas in a low voice so the driver wouldn't hear. "Or do you think they've already put me on a no-fly list?"

"Don't worry, everything will be fine," he said.

Both of us knew these were just empty words to comfort me. Many of the other journalists and activists in Egypt had already been banned from traveling. The question was, whose time was next?

We finally arrived at the airport, and I unloaded my two bags on the street. It was all I could hastily pack in ninety minutes. I looked at the airport building, then back to Cairo's skyline. I wondered if this would be the last time I set eyes on it.

How did it come to this? Why did I have to flee, while tyrants and thieves got to stay? I didn't steal, didn't abuse my powers, and certainly didn't hurt anyone. All I did was tell jokes.

I wheeled my bags through the terminal and then peeked at my boarding ticket.

Destination: Dubai.

Destiny: Unknown.

CLOSE
ENCOUNTERS
WITH A
REVOLUTION

We live in an era of instant gratification in which we crave meaning-less recognition: "shares" of our inflated achievements on Facebook, retweets of our 140 characters of fake wisdom on Twitter, and "likes" for the stupid photos of meals we are about to eat (and will inevitably shit out thirty-six hours later) on Instagram.

Instant gratification may be achieved from social media, but it really doesn't work the same way for revolutions. Imagine a revolution succeeding just because of the sheer number of shares, likes, or retweets. Wouldn't that be something?

On January 25, 2011, the Egyptian Revolution started. On February 11, 2011, Hosni Mubarak, the thirty-year dictator, stepped down.

Wait! Who the fuck is Hosni Mubarak? And isn't Egypt in Africa? Why the hell did you need an Arab Spring in Africa?

I know I said I wasn't going to give you a second-rate history lesson on the Middle East, but I've got to catch you up to speed at least a little bit. For many Americans, *Egypt*, *Muslim*, *Arabs*, *Africa* might not fit in the same sentence. The thing is, we are all that. (And much more, baby!)

Yeah, sure, our ancestors built the pyramids, and I know you've seen our pharaohs and gods make appearances in some of your blockbuster movies. Like when Australian actor Joel Edgerton was the *obvious* choice for Rameses II in that terrible movie *Exodus: Gods and Kings*. Or how about when Scottish actor Gerard Butler played Set (deity of chaos and war) in that piece of crap *Gods of Egypt*? The parade of moviemaking garbage goes on and on. Not to mention, we rarely even get credit for the amazing monuments our great-great-great-great-great-great-great-(you get the picture)-great-grandparents left behind. Typically, that glory goes either to the Jews or a bunch of aliens. But then when I see what decades of dictator-ships have done to my country I say to myself, *You know, maybe it wasn't us!* We are the African nation who thought it could do better but ended up doing nothing.

We don't speak "Egyptian" just like you don't speak "American." We are an Islamic country that speaks Arabic. And although we are a Muslim country, we do have a small population of Christians—so you can just think of us as a reverse United States, religion-wise. Also worth noting: we don't ride camels to work and our women aren't all belly dancers. A disappointment, I know.

Politically, we've gone from pharaohs to khedives (whatever the hell that means) to presidents. By the time we reached 2011, Hosni Mubarak was a third-generation president, essentially meaning he was the third president of Egypt since Egypt started a love affair with military regimes. Calling it a love affair is being generous, though, as it is more of a domestic abuse situation in which the wife is battered, bruised, and brainwashed into thinking that her husband "really loves her."

And it only took eighteen days to kick to the curb the dictator who ruled us for thirty years. Thirty years—also known in the Middle East as a "short first term"—was the life expectancy of our leaders in the Middle East.

You might find it strange or unusual but isn't that better than what we see in a backward Western democracy like the United States? You guys spent over $5 billion this past election just to get a president for four years? That's like throwing a massive new wedding for your spoiled-brat daughter every four years because she keeps marrying and divorcing rat-schmucks like Ted Cruz and Chris Christie. You really need to revisit how democracy should work, guys. I mean, after all this money-spending you wound up with Donald Trump.

In the Middle East assholes come for free.

You see, in the Arab world we need to make long-term plans, and we can't just change them every four years because of the uncertainty of something trivial like elections! We have to plan ahead for our vacations, commitments, and jail time. Your democracy won't really cut it for us. Plus, you got Trump as president, so you're really not in a postion to mock our "democracy" or our "choices" (even if we don't have any) of horrible leaders.

So back to us: we had an eighteen-day revolution and believed it worked. But no revolution really happens in eighteen days. Revolutions are like bloody, agony-inducing roller coasters that often end in fiery crashes of epic failure. So it seems we had the luxury of a short-term glory, but would spend the following five years paying our debt.

I often get pissed when I see some American talk shows discuss how "disappointed" they are that our revolution of eighteen days didn't work. This breed of Americans thinks that your Revolutionary War took the same time it took to shoot the movie *The Patriot*.

Prior to our revolution, I wasn't an activist or remotely involved in any kind of politics. I was a heart surgeon. Let that sink in: I used to cut open people's chests for a living.

By 2010, I had finished all my American medical-license exams and was desperately looking for a way out to work in the U.S. Honestly, I never really liked being a doctor. It was just a great line to open a conversation with a hot chick. The conversation usually didn't go anywhere because I sucked at talking to women, but as a doctor you get the added benefit of talking to women without them answering back while they are under anesthesia. Sick, I know!

I had my fantasies of becoming a worldwide star, maybe an actor. By some miracle I would win an Oscar and marry Jennifer Aniston in the process. But since there was no clear path on how to get there, I did the next best thing and became a nerd.

You see, I come from a typical middle-class family. My father was a judge, my mom was a university professor, and my older brother was an engineer. Having a son as a doctor or an engineer is a coveted social status. Since I hated numbers and biology made more sense to me, I went to medical school to complete the family portrait. Now my mother could brag about "my son the doctor and my other son the engineer." I know! We almost sounded like a Jewish family!

Even though I didn't like medicine, I tried to make the best of it. But working as a doctor in Egypt, in its ever-failing, underfunded, good-for-nothing health-care system, puts a lot of pressure on you. I thought if I could work as a doctor in a different country I would at least feel better about what I did. So I put my nerd power into overdrive and passed every single possible exam to get the hell out of there. I finally found an opening in Cleveland. I was excited that this might be my way out. Nothing can tell you how desperate

I was to get out of the country like my getting pumped about going to Cleveland. Basically, the way I felt about Egypt was the same way LeBron James felt about Cleveland when he moved to Miami. One man's Cleveland is another man's Miami.

Before 2011, I was politically apathetic. This is a normal feeling after having lived with the same president for thirty years. We were even waiting for Mubarak, the ailing dictator, to push his son into his place. It was something like the Bush and Clinton dynasties but without elections, transparency, competition, accountability, or . . . anything. If an Arab president decides his son is the next president, you can object, but it won't change anything. As a matter of fact, the dictator can be dead already and the powers that be will bring his son from London, change the constitution since the son is younger than the required age, and usher him into the presidency. That exact sequence happened in Syria with Bashar al-Assad, so why not with us?

When January 2011 came along, I was waiting for my visa papers to arrive from Cleveland when something radically unusual happened: hundreds of thousands of people took to the streets.

Where did all those people come from? There was a mix of young and old people, with a hodgepodge of beliefs, yet there were no religious slogans. No complicated chants. They were shouting, "Down, down, Hosni Mubarak."

There are many stories of why people took to the streets. Maybe the most circulated one was about a Facebook page calling for a demonstration dedicated to renouncing police brutality in the wake of a young student being tortured and killed by the police. (Careful, America!)

The other unofficial story was that the Arab Spring started in Tunisia, which inspired young people in Egypt. We were not going to be upstaged by this small puny motherfucking country called Tunisia. Egypt is way bigger, cooler, and older than Tunisia, obviously. So yeah, there is a high probability that we may have started our revolution because we were simply attention whores and drama queens. Call us the Kardashians of the political world.

If you were in the streets, it looked like an uprising, a revolution with thousands out there demanding their freedom and for Mubarak to step down. But the national networks refused to broadcast the unrest. There was a nationwide split personality disorder on display, in which two separate realities existed simultaneously: the brutal reality of the streets and the tranquil reality of the TV. According to the TV media, this was not a revolution but a conspiracy orchestrated by the CIA (Central Intelligence Agency), Mossad (Israeli national intelligence agency), Hezbollah (Lebanese Shi'a Islamist militant group), Hamas (Palestinian Sunni-Islamic fundamentalist organization), and maybe even the Village People (New York's super-gay disco group from the seventies).

Pundits were popping up all over the screen to tell us about the "American Zionist conspiracy" to bring down Egypt, citing evidence to support that Iran and Hamas were also involved. You can't make that shit up.

With all those nations and security and intelligence agencies getting together to conspire against us, you would think that the Egyptian Revolution had already succeeded in the one thing every contestant in every beauty pageant claims she wants to achieve: world peace.

"Those lovely youth in the streets don't know what they are getting themselves into," one pundit said. "Our Egyptian youth are falling victim to international conspiracies put into effect by our enemies." It was as if he was saying, *Whoops! Thousands of people just happened to accidentally take to the streets at the same time fundamentalist groups and counterintelligence agencies were looking to sabotage the Egyptian government.*

Sometimes, if you switched on the television you would see the cameras fixed on an empty bridge or a tranquil view of the Nile. One channel's producer was so dumb that on a day when the camera was fixed on one of those bridges, he didn't realize that at the top of the screen, on another bridge, huge clashes between protestors and security forces were taking place! News programming at its finest.

The protests heralded in a new chapter: the rich, the poor, the liberal, the Islamist, the Christian, all sharing this common space in Tahrir Square. For three days I watched the clashes on international news networks and didn't know what to make of it.

I was one of those people who saw the Tunisian dictator flee his country a few weeks before, and like many people I never thought the same thing could happen in Egypt. Tunisians are one of the most educated populations in the Arab world. On the other hand, Egypt has one of the highest illiteracy rates in the region. "Egypt is not Tunisia" was the most repeated phrase on television. I, like many other Egyptians, believed that sentiment. Deep inside we hated the regime, but after thirty years of political stagnation, we never thought that change could actually be possible.

AFTER THREE DAYS OF BEING CLEARED FROM THE STREETS BY the police, many protestors called for January 28 to be the "Day of Anger," in which the protestors proclaimed that they would not leave the streets this time.

On that day the government made quite possibly the worst decision possible: they shut down mobile phone service across the nation.

Now people with no communication would have to see for themselves what was happening in the square. News about masses of Egyptians pouring into the streets was circulating widely. My wife, Hala, whom I had married only a couple of months earlier, was scared. She fought with me because I wanted to go to the square. "Can't you see the clashes in the streets? I am not ready to be a widow yet!" she said.

So I stayed home with her and watched the BBC and Al Jazeera channels, which were broadcasting live. The security forces seemed adamant that no one would come into the square that day.

We witnessed something that we never thought we would see in our lifetime. Lines after lines of anti-riot police faced tens of thousands of protestors wanting to reach the square. The authorities considered this an ultimate standoff, where all bets were made or lost on those three hundred feet leading to the square. It was a scene that even Steven Spielberg couldn't come up with.

I kid, he can do anything!

After hours of clashes, endless amounts of tear gas, rubber bullets, and armored cars crushing protestors, it happened: hundreds of black-suited heavily armored men turned the other way and started running. We the People were chasing after the police! It was unbelievable to see it the other way round. The almighty face of authority fell right there and then. Decades of fear and awe inflicted by an authoritarian regime fell at the feet of the protestors, who ran over the police gear to take the square.

Millions like me decided to come down to the streets to see it with our own eyes.

We felt like we had entered a post-apocalyptic movie set. (Hey! Maybe it *was* Spielberg after all!) There was the heavy smell of gas from the clashes the night before mixed with the smoke rising from burned, well, everything: shops and cars were completely destroyed. People were dancing and singing on destroyed police armored vehicles. Others were preparing for a long sit-in by setting up makeshift hospitals, organizing places to stay, and handing out food, while looters took over the burned-out building of the ruling party. We saw people running away with office chairs and even AC units. The L.A. riots looked pedestrian by comparison.

As we approached the middle of the square, things were a little more organized. No looting or chaos there. Protestors were already setting up what would, in a few days, become the main stage. Checkpoints were being formed and huge banners prepared. The biggest of all read: THE PEOPLE DEMAND THE FALL OF THE REGIME. It rolls off the tongue a little better in Arabic.

And then, of course, there were photographers, news reporters, and television crews. I passed by an American reporter from ABC interviewing one of the men setting up the tents. She was having difficulty understanding his poor English. I volunteered to translate and her face lit up, as if to say, *Ohhh thank god, someone speaks our language.* I think I stole that guy's thunder, but it was time for me to make my TV debut. I can't remember what she asked me exactly, but I remember saying, "Mubarak has already fallen."

She was surprised and asked me, "Isn't it a bit premature for that assumption?"

"I don't know if what I am saying is making any sense or not," I replied. "I am no politician or analyst, but I think Mubarak will fall, will be captured, and will be put on trial."

Oh, how cute and delusional at the same time, her smile seemed to say, which left me with a feeling that I was either too optimistic or just plain stupid. The jury is still out.

My relationship with Tahrir Square over the next few days was a casual one. I didn't stay overnight but would visit every day, as my wife and I distributed food to the people staying there. Despite the festive mood inside the square, something else was happening on the outside. Hundreds of thugs started appearing everywhere along the roads leading to the square. These paid thugs were an effective weapon used by the police for the past thirty years. They were used to suppress minor demonstrations, so it would seem that a struggle between different factions of the people had occurred. These thugs were also used to scare voters from entering polling stations during elections. They would later be employed by the authorities to do their dirty work, without getting uniformed police involved—not to mention they would be the ones to attack my studio three years later. These thugs had had a name for years, and it was coined by the state-run media: "honorable citizens." Over the next couple of years we would become very familiar with their faces. You didn't need an officer in uniform to scare you. Fear came in many forms.

The thugs were stopping cars going to Tahrir, looking inside them to see if their occupants had any Egyptian flags. If flags were found, it could only mean that you were going there to celebrate with the "defectors." In the U.S., not standing for the flag is considered unpatriotic; in 2011, carrying the Egyptian flag could get you in trouble.

One day my wife and I drove toward the square, not carrying flags or banners in the car, but food supplies to offer to the people. We were stopped at a checkpoint controlled by those thugs when a guy came up to the car holding a thick stick. The scars on his face gave off a distinct "do not fuck with me" look.

"Where are you going?" he asked.

"We are going to Tahrir Square," I answered politely, as my wife's body shook.

He looked in the backseat and noticed the shopping bags. "What is this? Food? You better leave right now or else your car will be trashed."

We turned back, but managed to arrive at Tahrir through a more secure entrance, facilitated by the protestors.

For three days I divided my time between those visits and my work in the hospital. On one of those days, Mubarak appeared on TV to deliver a sentimental speech that actually made a difference.

He pledged that he would never run for president again, which caused many protestors to leave the square because they believed in his speech's emotional rhetoric. Still, many remained because they didn't trust the authorities or because they thought it was a trick, and that once they cleared the square they would all be arrested for treason.

It was early in the afternoon of February 2 when something bizarre happened as we watched the TV at the hospital: people with camels and horses started attacking the square. Not armored vehicles, not security forces, but fucking camels and horses. Now, I know I've already joked that Egyptians don't ride camels to work even though our region has been living in the seventh century, but this was just too much.

The "official" story was that workers around the pyramids and tourist sites were complaining that there were no more tourists because of the clashes and the unrest, so they went to Tahrir to protest the protests!

What had really happened was a full-on attack by tourist-site workers supported by hundreds of those "honorable citizens" thugs to disband the protestors. The regime was trying to tell the world that there were two sides to this conflict, and they weren't the people versus the regime; they were people versus people. However, one of the only reasons there were pro-Mubarak forces involved was because people were being bribed and coerced into supporting the authorities.

At this point, a decision was made by everyone at the hospital to go to the center of the action. The nurses prepared medical supplies, and before you knew it everyone had made their way to the clashes. The square, nearly empty that morning, was now full, as street wars erupted right there in the middle of Cairo.

Each section of Tahrir Square seemed to represent a different reality. There were the "war zones" on the periphery, where there was a constant exchange of rocks and Molotov cocktails; there were the areas right in the center, where people sang and danced like it was the Egyptian version of Woodstock; then there were parents coming to visit the square with their children to buy food from street vendors offering sandwiches and tea. The variety of action was absurd.

I remember the first time I went to the main clinic to check on those who had sustained injuries during the unrest. I spent around eight hours treating all kinds of injuries. Then, patients whom I'd stitched up headed directly back to the "firing line," only to return with fresh injuries.

I decided to leave the main clinic and make my way to some of the makeshift clinics on the periphery of the square, where I was only a couple of hundred meters from the hot zone. *If I am going to be in the middle of a revolution, why not witness the action from a better seat?* I told myself.

You should know that I am not a violent person. The last fight I was involved in happened in eighth grade, and I had my ass handed to me by a guy two years my senior. Years later, I decided to take up boxing, and six months into it I got a bad black eye in a practice fight with an Egyptian boxing champion. I'd like to say you should've seen the other guy, but he was fine. Violence is just not my thing. But now I was tempted to take an active role and join those brave demonstrators. So I approached the protestors on our side that were defending the square. They were holding huge sheets of metal taken from a construction site nearby to form barricades. I decided that this was it, my big chance to be a part of the resistance. I picked up a stone from the ground and walked a few steps closer to the front line. I gathered my courage, and really let it fly. That throw was emblematic of my inability to physically fight an enemy, because my hand slipped, and instead of projecting the stone over the barricades to hit our attackers, I threw it straight ahead, nearly hitting one of the protestors on our side. One guy looked back to check out who the fucking traitor was. Thankfully, I was wearing a white doctor's coat, which gave me some sort of moral status and deflected his suspicions. I turned the other way as innocently as possible and decided to continue treating injuries instead of causing them.

Up until the moment I treated one of those thugs, I didn't really understand why they were attacking the square, but then some protestors came over and asked me to verify a story told by one of the captured thugs.

"We just captured this man who is claiming that he is on kidney dialysis and he needs to leave or he will be very sick; can you verify that?" I was asked.

They led me to the entrance of the metro station, where they were keeping their "prisoners of war." The man cried out to let him go. I asked him how he had gotten involved in the first place and he told me a similar story told by most of the thugs there—that many of them were either addicts or poor and had been rounded up by senior thugs who gave them money to go and "purify" the square of the "traitors." Some of them mentioned the names of prominent figures from the ruling party.

I examined the guy and found that he was indeed on dialysis treatment. "When you have nothing to eat you will do anything for two hundred pounds," he told me.

I asked the protestors in charge to release him, which they did. They told me that every time they released someone to the army, however, the person would come back and attack the protestors again the next day.

At that time we still had faith in the army, though. We thought that when they took to the streets they were on our side or at least being neutral. However, looking back, while the thugs and their camels attacked the square, the armed forces never interfered. We were in denial (insert your own stupid "de-Nile" joke here) and refused to think too much about it. Back then, we thought that the army would never betray us. How stupid were we?

For everyone who visited, the square was a sacred, beautiful place, where a powerful regime was toppled through mostly peaceful resistance. It would take us a few months to see that the regime hadn't fallen, nor did the square maintain its sanctity.

SUPER-DIGITIZE ME

Let's go back a couple of steps to before all this happened. In Egypt before 2010, Internet basically consisted of Facebook and a few YouTube videos. There was no original Arabic content on it.

It was around this time that Tarek, an old friend of mine, graduated as an engineer and became one of the first people in Egypt to start managing YouTube content. Little did he know he was jump-starting a major trend.

For whatever reason he came to me in the summer of 2010 and told me that he wanted to produce original content and use me as a host.

"Why me?" I asked.

"Well, you have a way," he said. "When you talk, people listen. I think if I put a camera on you, people will watch."

"You are not using me for porn, are you?"

"I wish we had the women, bro," he answered. "I think you're a great choice for the Internet. Also, you are my friend. So I can use you without paying you."

I guess that settled it.

At that time, politics was really off the table. As a matter of fact, in 2001, before there was something called YouTube, a group of five young people made a video spoof of one of the most popular

Egyptian war movies. People were sharing it through videotapes and CDs and hard disks. Ultimately, all five people ended up arrested and interrogated by national security officers. They were eventually let go, but only after they confirmed they were just a bunch of stupid young men who didn't have any political agenda.

Since politics was off limits, I decided to make my video debut about a less controversial topic. Religion!

I was really asking for it.

I came up with a concept and settled on a title for the webisodes, *Searching for a God*. Each episode was about a religion or a cult; I would discuss and mock some of their wacko beliefs in five minutes or less.

This proves that I was ahead of Morgan Freeman by at least several years. I should sue him for stealing my idea with his new show *The Story of God*. Screw you, Morgan!

We shot three episodes and showed them to our friends, who loved the concept and the controversial content. I was already having dreams of fame, but at the same time was dying to work as a doctor in the States. Actually, I was dying to leave the country, and medicine was my only ticket out! So in my head I reached a fantasy compromise. I would travel to the U.S. and in a couple of years some huge TV exec would discover those episodes on the Internet and hire me as the host of a show who goes around the world to film actual cults in their native countries. I would be the Anthony Bourdain of religions: *Bassem Youssef: No Revelations*. End of fantasy.

We set the release date for *Searching for a God* for New Year's Eve 2011. But that night, a bombing occurred outside a Coptic Christian church in the heart of Cairo. Yup, that's how we celebrate Christmas in my part of the world. That's why when I see Bill O'Reilly ranting for hours on end about a "war on Christmas" or the sacrilege of no red cups at Starbucks, all I can say is "Bitch, please!"

Following that explosion we decided not to release the videos on YouTube, and postponed the whole thing for a few weeks. But twenty-five days later, all of a sudden we just happened to have a revolution—you know, that little thing I started telling you about—and we lost sight of the project. There was nothing else for the next few weeks other than the events of the uprising.

A week after Mubarak stepped down, Tarek called me. "Hey, forget about *Searching for a God* for now. We need a new project. Let's do something humorous and political. This is the best time for that kind of content."

"Great!" I said. "Then I want to do something like Jon Stewart." (Who, I should inform you, is my biggest inspiration.)

"What?" Tarek replied. "No one will get it. It won't work. Whatever, dude, just give me some content to put up there."

I started collecting available online material from the Egyptian mainstream media. The widespread backlash against the media rose with the release of each new YouTube video. Now that Mubarak had stepped down and the revolution had "won," those who had originally insinuated the revolution was a conspiracy, opposed it from the beginning, or instigated hate against it found themselves on a sort of public blacklist. The hypocrisy and deception we found in those videos was unmatched. They were full of paranoia, hate, lies . . . and lots of sex!

THE SEX ORGY REVOLUTION

With one camera, one desk, and one banner that cost a hundred dollars, we filmed in the laundry room of my apartment.

On March 8, 2011, we released the first five-minute episode on the Internet. It satirized how the media and celebrities tried to tarnish the protests in Tahrir Square.

"We should get rid of those protestors in Tahrir!" shouted a celebrity actor in the episode. "Why doesn't the army order a tank to advance in the square and shoot one shot? Just one shot in the air. The traitors will flee and only the good people of Egypt will stay."

A shot from a tank in the middle of Cairo? What could possibly go wrong? I'm sure a tank blast in the middle of Times Square would probably have a similar effect of separating the muggers from the good people of New York, right?

"I have been in Tahrir myself," added the same actor. "I was there in disguise. I saw everything. This is not a revolution. People were dancing, singing, using drugs, and engaging in complete sexual relations." Someone had actually used the phrase *complete sexual relations*.

Damn! Who knew the revolution was just a glorified frat party? Yet, for a nation with horny, sexually deprived youth, that image was the best motivation for more people to support the insurgence in Tahrir. If not for freedom, then at least for the hope of getting laid.

And I couldn't help but ask the question: If there are *complete* sexual relations, what are *incomplete* sexual relations? Is the man halfway in? Does the couple stop halfway through the act and smoke a joint? Do men who do not receive the whole "complete sexual relations" end up having blue balls?

You see, sex is a great talking point in our region. If you want to discredit a person, a cause, or a whole movement, you can just drop accusations related to sex. It is the ultimate taboo, but that doesn't stop us from topping most countries when it comes to PornHub.com searches. Maybe the next time Americans want to deal with a problem in the Middle East, they should send us strippers instead of troops. Middle East problem solved!

For my first episode I was hoping for about ten thousand views on YouTube, which would've been considered viral in Egypt. But in two days the video hit 100,000 views. In two months, the show's views increased to 5 million. This was truly unprecedented in the Arab world. (I know what you are thinking . . . *5 million? That is what my cat videos get now.* 2011, people, 2011.)

People shared my videos on Facebook and on Twitter. They started to recognize me in the street and stop me for photos. I was living a bizarre double life: working in the hospital during the week, and on the weekends editing and shooting the episodes.

The first videos were amateurish, but, still, they were a huge hit. People enjoyed seeing me taking the piss out of the celebrities and TV personalities who lied to them and betrayed the revolution. But it was not just the celebrities. The media narrative was worthy of Orwellian fiction. Big Brother was in control. And how does Big Brother drive masses? Simple.

Step 1: Create an enemy.

Step 2: Make sure it speaks English.

Step 3: Rinse and repeat.

ENGLISH AS A CRIMINAL LANGUAGE

A second language is usually a great addition to your résumé wherever you are. It improves your chances of getting hired and might take you to unforeseeable places. The same more or less applies in Egypt: speaking English in Egypt can improve your chances of getting arrested and visiting an Egyptian jail.

Egyptians are welcoming people when it comes to foreigners. After all, our habit of supplying tourist attractions is not just second nature, it is also important to the economy. Egypt needs your money (and not just in the form of military and economic aid!). But how does a foreign language change from being a way to communicate with tourists to a national security crisis?

Well, leave it up to Big Brother. Or as we call it, "our father in the intelligence." For more than six decades, Egypt was controlled by the military apparatus. They controlled everything—from security to the economy to the media. The Soviet Union might have died in the eighties, but it still lived in our region. Whenever the military intelligence felt threatened, foreigners were always an easy target to blame.

We were first aware of the dangers of the English language by way of a video that I had used in one of my earliest online episodes. It became an iconic landmark, showing the way state-run propaganda operates.

Referred to as "Weeping Tamer," this video shows a young man named "Tamer" calling in to one of the TV news bulletins on the government channel. In a teary voice he describes how he joined the masses in the streets in good faith, but now he wants to repent because he has discovered the evil plots behind this so-called revolution.

"Can you please tell us what you saw that made you reach this conclusion?" asks the anchor.

"These people are not Egyptians, they are not from here. They want to destroy the country," explains Tamer, his crying taking up most of his conversation.

"Yes, but can you please tell us what you saw?" asks the anchor again.

"These people are weird and they speak English very, very well."

(I remember translating that video for an American friend of mine, and his response was: "Where the fuck were those people when I was asking directions to the pyramids?")

That was enough to plant the first seeds of doubt in the hearts of people watching the revolution from home.

Many calls from other alleged "Weeping Tamers" came flooding in. The story was more or less the same. Young men drawn into the revolution now saw the light. They claimed they were tricked by external powers and their operatives, who could speak perfect English.

After Mubarak stepped down we learned that the original "Weeping Tamer" was actually a network employee who was patching in from the control room as part of a staged phone call.

These phone calls were now a comical yet disheartening reminder of how media manipulated people at the time. During the uprising in those eighteen days, people who didn't understand or support the revolution also didn't realize that behind the scenes a covert operation was taking place to further implicate foreigners. Egyptian television was busy interviewing proud Egyptians who had captured and turned in foreigners of all nationalities.

"We found two people walking on the bridge," said one citizen to a mainstream media source. "When they didn't give a good answer for why they were just walking around like that we turned them in to the army. They turned out to be Irish."

Actually, I could believe that. Only the Irish would be drunk enough to walk around in the middle of the night in a Middle Eastern country while the largest unrest in its history was occurring!

A celebrity singer called in and claimed that he and some of his neighbors had just captured two "Swiss Islamists." Now, this is a scenario that's very hard to imagine. Were they yodeling about their radical neutrality? Was Switzerland invading us with scrumptious chocolates? But these were not mere rumors. To many citizens of Egypt, this was strong evidence that foreigners were involved in the revolution. State-run media showed videos and photos of foreigners *in the middle of Tahrir* dancing with the protestors. Of course, it may be worth mentioning that one of the biggest tourist spots, the Museum of Egyptian Antiquities, is just two hundred yards away from the square. Imagine retired, senile tourists walking out of the museum to find themselves in the middle of a revolution that was not exactly a part of their predetermined travel tour. But why not get a free treat and take in some of the local fare? Or you could believe that these dim-witted white folks who just happened to be in Egypt checking off an item on their bucket list were highly trained coverts. I mean, it's your choice.

Egypt is a tourist destination, and the authorities were shooting themselves in the foot by denying this. As a matter of fact, in the next few years the government would move from capturing tourists to killing them with fighter jets in the desert; stick around, more of that to come. To them, national security was of the upmost priority. It didn't matter if you alienated foreigners or Egyptians themselves, the country came first, even at the country's expense. It didn't matter how ridiculous the claims were. Like when the nine o'clock news proudly announced the arrest of fifty Eritreans and thirty-five Ethiopians for espionage!!! Even our African brothers were on to us!

The bottom line is, the state-run media were doing a great job of making it appear that everybody was against the revolution. And they had no better weapon than the source of all evil—the one we love to hate and hate for loving—the Satan we all admire. The mighty US of A.

AMERICA: WE LOVE TO HATE YOU

When people in the West ask me how we Arabs, Muslims, and Middle Eastern folks feel about America, I sum it up like this: "We hate your guts, but we would kill to get your visa."

America was cited as the reason for everything evil that happened during the revolution: The revolutionaries accused America of supporting Mubarak and not moving fast enough to get him out. And the media accused America of staging the whole Arab Spring to destabilize the region. When they produced "evidence" that some of the revolution's leaders were paid operatives, there were calls pouring in on TV outing the fact that many of the so-called revolutionaries and the thousands of people taking to the streets were only protesting because they were paid $50 and given a bucket meal from KFC. It only makes sense that fake protestors were bolstered with food from a fake chicken colonel. How finger-lickin' American!

What Western think tanks get wrong all the time is that they believe they can actually figure out how we feel about America through geopolitical, socioeconomic, and cultural bullshit. This will never work; their best bet is to hire a therapist to analyze us.

In the 1950s and 1960s under President Gamal Abdel Nasser, our first ever military dictator, Egypt was leaning toward the Soviet camp of communism, so of course we hated America. The U.S. had always supported Israel, vetoed every single Security Council resolution against them, and turned a blind eye every time they bombed the shit out of the Palestinians. Everyone had their reasons to hate America: Islamists, the military, leftists, liberals, and even poor taxi drivers. America is an easy target toward which to direct your hate in Egypt. If you are a leader and can't run the country properly, just convince the people that America is ruining everything. America is the devil for the Islamists because it wants to defeat Islam. We are enormous hypocrites, though, because while America empowers and financially assists Israel—our biggest enemy—we, at the same time, receive some of the largest chunks of American military aid. Meanwhile, Egyptian leftists hate America because it represents everything ugly about capitalism and world domination, while secular elitists hate America because it has empowered the extreme religious monarchies in the gulf region (who ironically sponsor the extreme religious scholars who tell the people that America is fighting Islam). And . . . the poor taxi driver hates America because he gets denied a visa to get away from all these crazy people.

Nonetheless, this despised America is a dream destination for many of Egypt's hypocrites. Some of the most outspoken opponents of America send their kids to American schools and universities. When these people get sick, they travel to get treated in America. Their vacation retreats are mostly in the U.S. and Europe—all paid for by the money they sucked from the poor people of Egypt while telling them that the reason they are poor is America.

America and Israel are the excuses for all failures and government incompetence. I wouldn't really mind if Egypt actually manned up and had a serious hate-fueled relationship with them, but when it disses America and Israel while lying in bed with them for financial, security, and political arrangements, we really just come off like assholes.

It is an interesting relationship in a country where people illegally download the latest episodes of *Breaking Bad* and *Game of Thrones* and fill the movie theaters for the latest *Avengers* movie. If Americans only knew how lucky they are that their endless lines are at Disney World while ours are queues in front of the American embassy.

THE DAY THE REVOLUTION ENDED
(PART 1)

Many think the revolution ended in 2013, when the military took over (yeah, we will come to that). Some think that it ended before that, when Islamists got hold of the country in 2012 (I promise we will get to that too!). In my opinion, the revolution ended only nine weeks after Mubarak stepped down.

Mubarak's rule was centered on one principal message: "Either me or absolute chaos." He made everyone believe that if he stepped down Islamist extremists would win over Egypt and create another Afghanistan. This wasn't new; throughout the Arab world military dictators used this message as a tool to stay in power. This is why Western powers had no problem with Mubarak or other military leaders or dictators in the Middle East. For them, the likes of Mubarak represented "stability," which is another word for taking care of America's interests in a discreet way without having to deal with public outcry. It's similar to the way America supported many dictators in Latin America to protect its interests from communists. That's why Castro was a real mind fucker: he was both a dictator and a communist.

For Mubarak to maintain his position as the "only" option, he had to destroy any liberal or moderate opposition while keeping Islamic political power on a tight leash, and, as such, there was no other alternative in case of his departure than bringing in Islamists.

Mubarak officially stepped down on February 11, 2011, at which point the army took over for an interim rule and promised to hold elections the next year. But the army decided to quickly push a referendum vote on March 19. On the surface, they made it look like the people were being given an opportunity to choose how the presidential office and constitution would operate moving forward. Quite simply, though, the referendum fucked up the beautiful mosaic that was the revolution. It showed the ugly face of political Islam and alienated many people from the idea of democracy.

However, I really can't go on explaining why Egypt is such a clusterfuck without explaining what the hell Sharia Law is or who makes up the various Islamist parties. So get ready for the worst explanation of political Islam and Sharia you may ever encounter. It may not be good enough to help you pass your Middle Eastern politics class, but it'll do just fine for telling off your ignorant uncle at Thanksgiving.

LESSON ONE: SHARIA LAW

In my futile attempt to explain political Islam I will have to use the word *Sharia* a lot. Now, if you think you know what the hell it is, think again. We Muslims—all one and a half billion of us—have yet to really agree on what this word means.

A very stripped-down explanation is that Sharia is a collection of rules and laws that are inspired by the Quran. It includes the stories and traditions of the Prophet Muhammad, in addition to many rulings on Islamic law and interpretations from what theologists concluded after the Prophet.

For most people, their daily lives are dictated by Sharia and how it outlines the honorable way to approach issues like marriage, inheritance, charity donations, prayer, dietary rules such as abstaining from drinking or eating pork and making sure that the meat you eat is *halal* (kosher), and how not to be an asshole. Other followers extend Sharia to mandate how women should dress, the length of a man's beard, and how to be a real asshole to other "followers" whom they deem less religious.

Many take it even further and consider Sharia to be the undisputed law of God—including every single literal order and mandate of Sharia that has been in place for hundreds of years. They have taken ahold of Sharia's dogma by denying any attempts or interpretations to modernize the traditions. This is akin to applying the Bible's Old Testament as it was written. Could you imagine if your current boss forced all female employees to work in a completely separate office while they were menstruating because they were too "unclean" to mingle with men? How about stoning to death or beheading kids who cursed at their parents?

There are about fifty countries in the world with Muslim majorities. Many of them have Sharia Law as part of their constitution. And yet not everyone follows the literal or the most extreme interpretations. If you surveyed Muslims, the majority will say they prefer operating under Sharia Law, but this doesn't mean they would want to live under ISIS or al-Qaeda, which allegedly follows the most extreme interpretations. Just like many Americans could agree to live by the spirit of the Ten Commandments, but wouldn't want to take the religious right's doctrine as national law.

What makes it confusing is that different groups of people choose whatever interpretation fits them best. Which interpretation wins out really depends on who has the power and the money to impose it. The Saudis are rich and have a lot of money to spread around, so their interpretation, the most extreme, Wahhabism one, takes all the marbles.

I once had a heated discussion with a pro-Sharia Islamic scholar. He claimed that there is nothing wrong with Sharia, and that we as Muslims should apply the best possible version. I asked him which Sharia he wants to apply. Which Islamic country now or even in the past fifteen hundred years applied the best version of Sharia? And which religious scholars should carry that task? The ones in Saudi Arabia? The ones in Egypt? The ones in Iran? Indonesia, Malaysia, Algeria, Morocco? Which ones? He failed to answer.

If you go back to the 1940s, '50s, and '60s, the scary image of terrorist Muslims shouting "Sharia" is nowhere to be found. So how did that fucked-up version make a comeback?

America's archenemies, the Taliban, were on America's good side when the CIA was funding and arming them to beat the Soviet invasion of Afghanistan. Even Hollywood loved the mujahideen guerrilla militia types. That was obvious in *Rambo 3*. Do you remember this movie? It's so bad, it's good. It's where your all-American hero goes to Afghanistan to help the heroic mujahideen against the horrible, good-for-nuthin' Ruskies. A few years later, the real Soviet Union suddenly collapsed and the American media needed a scarecrow, and we stepped in to fill the gap. News agencies, you're welcome!

Okay. So, as I was saying, for decades the worst and most extreme interpretation of Sharia was fueled by Saudi money and their Wahhabi ideology. America goes along with it as long as they pump out the oil as fast as they pump the hate. But to be fair, it's not just Saudi Arabia. Many of the military regimes in the region love Sharia. You can't drive the masses with guns and tanks forever so you need a more spiritual controlling tool: the Good God Himself.

Sadat, our president before Mubarak, changed the constitution in 1980 to give himself unlimited presidential terms. And to pass this statute he also had to make a drastic change in the constitution to appease the Muslim majority. He tweaked the Sharia article in the constitution to state that instead of "Sharia is *a* source of legislation," "Sharia is *the* source of legislation." It is a wonder how a couple of letters can fuck a whole country.

A few months later he was assassinated during a victory parade, and Mubarak later took full advantage of the unlimited-terms article, allowing the Sharia clause to remain.

Now, Egypt's law doesn't allow beheadings, the removal of limbs, or the enforcement of many of the Wahhabi interpretations. But, when needed this article can be used to oppress free thinkers, minorities, or *anything* that is considered a threat.

The military would use Sharia to show that they are the guardians of religion and at the same time would let extreme radicals talk freely about their dream to apply an ISIS-like Sharia to scare everyone. It was the good old "it's either me or chaos/terrorism/ Jihad/etc." line.

Most people (including authorities) who identify as Islamists and who call for Sharia and "God's rule" are fucking hypocrites. An Arab philosopher once said, "If Muslims were given a choice to vote for either a secular or a religious state they would vote for the religious state and flee to live in the secular one." We are too afraid of some ephemeral God to vote in our own self-interest.

With this horrible and confusing explanation of one of the most used and abused words in today's Islamic discourse, now let's ask the next impossible-to-answer question: What the hell is political Islam?

LESSON TWO: A CRASH COURSE IN POLITICAL ISLAM

It is true that my story is about comedy and satire and how it managed to equally offend everyone in the middle of political turmoil. But I really can't tell the story without giving you a background of the key players in this region. Let's be real: If I started to talk about the Muslim Brotherhood and how they came to power and the jokes I made about them, you won't really get it if you don't know who the hell the Muslim Brotherhood are. It would be like making fun of the inane "Mexicans are all rapists and thieves" comment without explaining to a non-American the Dumpster fire that is Donald Trump.

Let's just start with the word *Islamist*. What is the difference between this word and *Muslim*?

Muslim refers to someone who belongs to the Islamic religion. That's easy. *Islamist*, on the other hand, describes someone or a group of people who use the religion as part of their political doctrine. You could be Muslim like me but hate the Islamists. There are two main subgroups in Egypt that fall under the Islamist category: the Muslim Brotherhood and the Salafis. When I use the word *Islamist* it will probably mean both of these groups, or those who belong to that camp of political Islam.

Good luck with that.

Now, let's move on . . .

The Muslim Brotherhood are by far the most important player when it comes to political Islam in Egypt. The Brotherhood began in the 1920s as a social movement that encouraged people to "get back to Islam" and be better Muslims, but soon developed into a political movement. There are all kinds of books and studies about the Muslim Brotherhood that describe their ideologies, rules, and social impact, so if you want a deeper look at their history, drop this book right now and get one of those boring books written by some scholar in Washington. *I don't do fair political analysis.*

I like to think of them as a cult-like group. (See? This is political science through feelings and impressions!) The Brotherhood has their own Joseph Smith–like character who founded the group in the 1920s, whom they don't think of as a prophet or anything, but whom they quote sometimes more than the Prophet Muham-mad. They think of themselves as better than everyone else because they alone know what "true Islam is." Isn't that too familiar? Basi-cally, they are the kids in class sitting in the first row sucking up to the teachers by reminding them to give the class more homework. I know, bunch of dicks, right?

Throughout their history, the Brotherhood had a habit of boot-kissing the authorities in order to push a religious narrative to the masses, and then finding themselves getting screwed by it. When Egypt had a king, the Brotherhood leaders were always on his side when he opposed the liberal opposition. Then, as the king grew un-comfortable with them, he ordered the assassination of their "Joseph Smith." When Nasser came to power in 1952, the Brotherhood ap-plauded him for crushing the workers' strikes and other political players, but their leaders ended up in Nasser's prisons, and some were even executed. Consider it a thank-you note from Nasser for all their hard work. During Mubarak's era, the Brotherhood's youth came out from universities to chant against Israeli occupation and advocate for the boycotting of American goods, but they would stifle chants coming from non-Brotherhood members who verbally as-saulted Mubarak.

This was the same Mubarak who would again send many of their leaders to prison and allow some of them to run for parliament. Crazy, right? The sadomasochistic relationship between the Muslim Brotherhood and the military makes *Fifty Shades of Grey* look like a nursery rhyme.

After the January 25 revolution, the Brotherhood were the military's bitches—in bed with them and applauding the military defamation of liberal opposition. That is until the military kicked the Brotherhood out of their bed and into the prisons (as we will see later).

The Muslim Brotherhood used the slogan "Islam is the solution," which was like a magical potion for their political campaign. They were evangelists for bringing back the Islamic caliphate (essentially an area that is ruled by a "chosen" religious leader, or caliph). People really bought into that. There is hardly a Muslim kid who didn't have his dream of dominating the world again and people converting to Islam right, left, and center. In the past few years since the Brotherhood came to power and started to impose their thinking, people in Egypt looked more into our history and read more about that caliphate. They found out that the utopian picture we had about our Islamic history is not entirely true. It was a history of colonization and wars, with bright spots of civilization as well as many dark moments of human stupidity. Really, the caliphate was like any other culture or empire and, more important, a far cry from the "divine" image Islamists loved to spread.

The Brotherhood managed to present themselves as the educated, modern Muslims of the moderate and non-violent variety. Although they may dress and appear nicer than your everyday ISIS-like radical Islamists, their history and continued shady behavior proved they still had a fucked-up mentality.

The other major player in our history and election was the Salafis, who are the real radical Islamists. If the Muslim Brotherhood were Southern Baptists, the Salafis were the Westboro Baptist Church. They took extremism to a whole new level.

The modern Salafi movement of Egypt began in the 1970s, when Sadat (our president before Mubarak) encouraged Islamic factions to come back to power in order to counteract the rising leftist youth movement in universities. He called himself the "pious" president—making it easier for him to pose as a divinely led leader. With more Egyptians finding work in Saudi Arabia and with the huge funding of the Saudi government, the Salafi movement found a place in Egypt.

Salafis were used like puppets by the military regimes to pacify the public. The more religious the people were, the more politically apathetic they would become. And since the Salafi sheikhs were under the control of the Egyptian equivalent of the NSA, Egyptian citizens were strategically pushed away from the intellectual and political sphere and into religious states that viewed the world as a dirty, unholy place. And when everyone is high on religion it's pretty easy to make them believe just about anything.

Side note: The word *sheikh* in Arabic literally means "old man." However, it is used in a multitude of ways. Most commonly it means men who are dedicated to teaching or preaching theology (the equivalent of a priest or a reverend). However, they come in many shapes and forms, and in the Middle East we are cursed with the worst kind of scumbags who use religion for political and power gains. In this book you will meet a lot of them.

The Egyptian regime during Mubarak made perfect use of this tool. They had home-grown many of the Salafis or reimported the Egyptian sheikhs who had gone to Saudi Arabia. They were the best weapon against the Muslim Brotherhood. You would think that both would work together, right? Islamists are all the same, right? Oh, hell no!

During Mubarak's reign, the Salafis and Muslim Brotherhood hated each other. As mentioned before, Salafi sheikhs were under the control of the Egyptian NSA. The Salafis promoted the idea that the Muslim Brotherhood was an abomination to Islam because it was a political faction. After the revolution those barriers fell and the Muslim Brotherhood and the Salafis somehow came to work together as one front. Nothing could bring two right-wing groups together quite like the common belief that no person should ever experience the freedom of thought.

I watched that transformation take place firsthand. My online videos were making me a bit more famous, and different political powers started approaching me because, I guess, they thought it was good to be on the side of a comedian. I would meet young, educated men from the Muslim Brotherhood who, in their perfect English, would tell me about how open-minded they were. It was obvious they had received their education at American universities, and they wanted to ease my worry about the supposed "Islamic tsunami" that was coming.

"Don't listen to the media," the Brotherhood members would tell me. "It's a new era, we really should all work together for a better future and coexistence."

The very next day their leaders would hold a joint rally with the Salafis in some poor neighborhood where they would announce that "the only way to govern is through Sharia law."

I would call the guy I was just sitting with the day before and would ask how he had justified that change of heart.

"It was taken out of context," he would answer.

Out of context, my ass!

We started to hear a whole new tone in the Brotherhood media. There were now channels dedicated solely to Islamist content. This in itself was not new; we had religious channels for years before that. But two things had happened: now those channels had primarily political agendas, and there were far too many of them.

Watching these channels, I felt as if the 700 Club and Fox News had merged to create a super-right-wing politico-religious Transformer. It was like a Sean Hannity wet dream come true, only with a different religion.

After a revolution that called for democracy, it was strange to hear people talking about democracy as a filthy by-product of the infidel West. "Unchecked democracy is *haram*," some of the Islamist leaders would announce. *Haram* means "forbidden" in Arabic.

The Salafi sheikhs were the first to go up against the revolution and issue *fatwas* declaring that what was happening in Tahrir was haram. Fatwas are rulings on Islamic law as determined by established leaders. Basically, it's like when you're playing a game and some jerk decides to reinterpret the rules right in the middle so he can win. One of the most famous fatwas used was: "It is forbidden to go out and topple the ruler because this will lead to chaos." And as we all know, God hates chaos.

But now the road was wide open for those Salafis to assume power, albeit with a dilemma. The revolution is haram but because of it, the people are free to elect a leader. How could the Salafis tell their followers to embrace the Muslim Brotherhood as political partners after issuing conflicting fatwas against them?

Well, the beautiful thing about fatwas is that they can be tailor-made. Every sheikh has his own supermarket of fatwas that allows him to justify and even reverse previous positions. So if you took this mentality and had followers who were willing to believe whatever bullshit you tell them, it is easy to assert that politics is no longer haram. The revolution is not haram either. The liberal youth were merely a tool to push the Salafi vision. Due to the results of the revolution coupled with their new political power, the Salafis could finally create their coveted Islamic State. The Muslim Brotherhood should no longer be seen as an abomination, but as the Salafis' brothers who could help achieve that goal.

After the fall of Mubarak, those two wings marked the beginning of the decline of the revolution toward Islamic fundamentalism. But to achieve their goals the Islamists needed a defining battle, an epic victory, or quite simply a referendum.

THE DAY THE
REVOLUTION
ENDED
(PART 2, OR WHY WE SHOULD ALL FUCKING
LEAVE AND GO TO CANADA)

So now that you have a very simple, inaccurate, and totally subjective idea about the different sects of political Islam in Egypt, let's continue.

Right after the revolution we were all on a high note celebrating the unity of the Egyptian people. Many imagined a secular country that contained us all. We could not have been further from the truth.

The army, now in charge of the country, had just announced that we would have a referendum concerning the constitution. It was a simple yes-or-no vote: if you wanted the old constitution but with a few amendments, you voted yes; if you wanted the constitution to be totally scraped and exchanged for a new constitution, you voted no.

A simple yes-or-no vote turned ugly. Most of the so-called liberal or civil figures called for a new constitution, for a no vote. Many of us changed our profile photos on Facebook to *No* images.

On the other side, the Islamists (both Salafis and Muslim Brotherhood) were endorsing the yes vote, employing one major strategy: they started to send their sheikhs and imams to the poorer places in Egypt to tell everyone that a no vote means a no against Islamic Sharia. You see, the old constitution had Islamic Sharia as one of the sources of legislation (remember Sadat and how one single word fucked us over?). Hysterical sheikhs started to tell everyone that liberals and seculars were plotting to strip Egypt of its Islamic identity and that a no vote was a vote against God.

We were just curious why those Salafi sheikhs who had basically been created by the regime to deter people from political activity were suddenly preaching to push people into a certain political direction.

Nevertheless, we had no doubt that the outcome would be an overwhelming no vote. How did we know? Well, because all my friends on Facebook had changed their profile photos to a big *No*. How could we lose? Also, we had all those liberal famous figures appearing in black-and-white videos on social media urging people to vote no. How can you lose when you have celebrities on your side? Same as when Trump won despite all of those celebrities, like Robert De Niro, actively campaigning against him. If you guys lose with the Godfather himself on your side . . . Well, the world does belong to assholes.

We discovered that not everyone in Egypt lives on Facebook. It turned out that a sheikh giving Friday prayer sermons in remote villages was more effective than all of social media and the liberal media combined.

When the results came in, nearly 80 percent of the vote was yes, which gave enough steam to Islamists to flex their muscles. Soon after the wonderful portrait of our revolution for unity, equality, and coexistence, we were split into two camps. The Islamists (the Muslim

Brotherhood and their new buddies, the Salafis) now thought that an overwhelming yes vote on the referendum was an overwhelming yes to totalitarian Islam.

The army could not have been happier. The result of the referendum was a repeated slap to the faces of those liberal powers who thought they could change the country. The army never wanted change, not with so many interests, businesses, and powerful people involved. It was a system sixty years in the making. Removing Mubarak didn't even touch the deep state that he was a disposable face of. The Muslim Brotherhood were never serious about the revolution either. They used it simply to come into power. They had no problem with the old regime as long as they were on top of it.

One of their most famous Salafi sheikhs, who pushed the narrative of "this is our country, not yours anymore," was Hussein Yacoub. He was an elderly man with bright blue eyes and a white beard like Santa Claus. One of his favorite pastimes was to marry four teenage girls at a time. Prior to the 1990s, when sheikhs like this guy rose to fame, the Salafis told their followers that television was haram. Most modern technology was haram—such as taking a photograph of yourself or owning a satellite dish, a "portal for Satan" to enter our houses. The idea was that if it didn't exist in the time of the Prophet Muhammad, then it was a novelty that we should not accept.

In the 2000s religious television was a huge business, and large sums of money were pushed into these channels. Not surprisingly, Salafi sheikhs were invited to host religious programs on television, which was supposed to be haram. But who cares when the money comes flowing in?

Yacoub was a perfect example of those scumbag sheikhs. He shifted from "TV is haram" to being the highest-paid Islamic televangelist. He was one of the people who pushed for a yes vote everywhere, and when he got it he said, "If you don't like the result, you should just leave the country and emigrate to Canada."

Canada had always been a destination for Egyptian Christians, or Copts, as they are called. He and many others insinuated that this vote was a victory over the Coptic Church and over the sinful liberals. Canada seems to be a refuge destination for everyone who gets screwed in elections, aka *losers*. I don't know how long Canada can keep taking people in. Whether from our part of the world or from you, America.

My seventh YouTube episode about the referendum was a no-brainer; it was, after all, the talk of the whole nation. I just had one problem. I wanted to make fun of one of the sheikhs, but how? Those people were essentially considered saints. Over the centuries, Muslims had raised these sheikhs to a level that if you dared talk against them or ridicule their opinion, you would be considered an Islam hater or, even worse, an "apostate."

Until then, many people suspected I was secretly Christian. Probably because I don't have three Mohameds in my name. And yes, in a country infested with radical Islamic views, being Christian could be considered very wrong by the general public. People who doubted my Muslim identity had their suspicions confirmed when I continued going after fanatic religious idiots.

Then, one day, a Christian church was burned down because word got out that a Muslim girl had converted to Christianity and went into hiding there. A lesser-known sheikh instigated hate against the "dirty Christians" who "take our daughters and fool them into Christianity."

I made fun of and ridiculed this asshole who was behind burning the church. I also made fun of some other sheikhs who were instigating hate.

According to them, I was clearly taking the side of the Christians, which means I had sinned. As my fans grew in number so did the number of people who hated me. But all of these YouTube videos were essentially the little leagues. There was nothing that would have prepared me for my next step: network television.

That's where the real hate begins.

HI, MOM!
I'M ON TV!

The unexpected and unprecedented popularity of my YouTube show had made me the hottest ticket in town. Six different television channels called, wanting to sign me on. This was a nice change of pace from the calls I used to get when people were going into cardiac arrest. Most of those channels just wanted to buy me out cheaply. They thought, *Well, here's an unknown from the Internet, surely he will just be happy to be on television.* I saw through their front and refused to be made host of some slap-dicked-together dog and pony show. As an avid follower of Arab television and as someone who knew the horrible quality it presented, I couldn't see myself repeating the same mistakes I'd seen others make. The channels thought that I was arrogant when I didn't accept their offers, but I decided that if I was going to do this, I would do it right and with a decent budget. In other words, if I was going to sell my soul, the price better be right.

I didn't know what was going on in the media business. The only people I knew from the media field were the people who started this with me from day one in the laundry room: Tarek (the guy who came up with the Internet production concept), Amr (my executive producer and a friend of Tarek), and Khalifa (my director and a friend of Amr). But they were basically nobodies in the world of media. They had no track record except for sporadic work here and there. Tarek just wanted to sell the idea and go on to find another YouTube sensation. Despite all of this, we were telling big-time channels that the only way to sign us on was if we were given the power to produce the show and manage the budget. Channel after channel walked away.

One day we got a call from the manager of a relatively new channel called ONTV, an independent station that was one of the best covering the events of the revolution. They offered a decent budget that was good for an unknown, but was not enough to do a decent show. We asked for triple the original number, which upset the manager of the channel enough to almost make him cancel the deal. But then the owner of the channel, one of the richest men in Egypt, called. We were invited to his office for a brief meeting.

"I like you and I like what you do," he told me. "I don't think we will get any profit out of you. But I think it is an experiment we should support."

He told the channel manager to make it happen. The manager thought that the owner was forced into the deal, so he changed the contract from a two-year to a one-year contract. I am proud to say that in one year's time he would come to greatly regret that decision.

So here I was in May 2011, just three months after I accidentally landed on YouTube, standing in the conference room of the channel with a contract in my hand. At that exact moment, my wife called. "The papers from Cleveland arrived!" she exclaimed. It was the opportunity I had been chasing for the past couple of years. I realized that my fate could literally be held in my two hands: a contract for a TV show in one and the papers to continue my medical career overseas in the other. It was a simple choice between a life of empty stardom, fame, and money . . . or saving lives. Of course I chose the money! It was a pretty okay price to sell my soul for.

You would think that my parents would've been heartbroken to watch me put medicine aside and choose media. But my mom was a typical Arab woman who would've hated seeing me cross the Atlantic Ocean and leave her. And by typical I don't mean the exhausted stereotypes of women wearing black potato sacks from foreheads to pinkie toes depicted in Indiana Jones movies. She was a strong, powerful university professor who incited fear in both her students and her family, if we ever made her angry. She was the most loving and dedicated person I have ever known and yet she was the person you didn't dare cross. She, like any other Middle Eastern woman, had only two tasks in life: one, to spend most of her life trying to get her kids married, and two, spend the rest of her life worrying about them. For her it was preferable that I stay in Egypt and pursue the television career, so long as I continued on as a faculty member at the medical school and she could still say "my son, the doctor (who just happens to do a little TV show on the side)."

THE FANS OF MY YOUTUBE SHOW HAD MIXED FEELINGS ABOUT MY move to television. Many thought my five-minute episodes were some sort of a statement against media corporations, a rebellious act against the establishment. I was the revolution hippie figure, a Guy Fawkes type taking on the Man, but without a mask.

Loyal fans started posting "How could you betray us?" comments on my YouTube and Facebook pages. To some, my going mainstream was a controversial and unexpected move. People who watched me on YouTube wanted to maintain ownership of the product they helped to succeed. They wanted me to continue doing YouTube videos, no matter how much it was costing, without providing any income for me or my team.

Many, however, were happy that I would be a regular on television.

But there will always be the haters. Not to mention one tiny detail that created a bit of an uproar: the owner of the channel was a Christian.

The fact I was going to a channel with a Christian owner was enough to "crucify" me (pun intended) all over Islamic social media. Skeptics were now dead sure that I was a Christian operative or a Muslim apostate who was financed by the anti-Islamic powers in order to ridicule Islam and Muslims. The more "reasonable" dissenters assumed that my hiring was a reward for my last two videos, where I made fun of their asshole sheikhs. Reasonable, right?

What made this situation worse was the way the billionaire station owner, Naguib Sawiris, behaved. Sawiris had a tendency to speak off the cuff during interviews. Many of his remarks would be taken out of context, allowing the media to play over and over again what appeared to be clips of him insulting Islam. If you can imagine a Christian pimp speaking through his diamond-encrusted grill while donning giant gold crucifixes and a puffy fur coat—that's what my employer looked like in the eyes of many Islamists.

Another issue that wasn't helping was Sawiris's political stance. You have to remember that Mubarak was president for thirty years. Under a dictatorship like that, you had to play nice and give compliments to the president every now and then. What made Sawiris different was that when the revolution started, his channel was one of the few that was balanced in its coverage and showed images of what was really occurring in the square.

Even I thought he was walking on thin ice at the time, and had the revolution failed to oust Mubarak he very well could have been one of the first to be executed.

Given his public persona it was difficult for me to know how to respect him as my employer without giving the Islamists more fuel for their fires. The Islamist social media had actively succeeded in creating this general theme of "Sawiris, the Antichrist," or in our case, "the anti-Muhammad"—and even if he was fairly open-minded, his image was already predetermined.

So I did what any good satirist would do and made fun of him. It was the first time that someone openly made fun of his boss like that on television. I know you guys in America think, *Okay, what's the big deal?* Well, here, where we have an authoritarian, patriarchal society, it was a huge deal. Sawiris was such a good sport about it, which put him in positive light for many. But as we all know, assholes will be assholes. The only way I could have satisfied those assholes' kind of hate would have been to physically cut Sawiris's throat right there in the studio.

Now that I was in the big leagues, I had to find myself a new team. Essentially, I wanted a simpler version of Jon Stewart's *The Daily Show.* When I tried to explain to my then small staff the type of show I wanted to create, they looked at me like I was crazy because no Egyptian show of that kind had ever been produced before.

I needed someone to help me make my ideal show come true, a sort of head captain. That's when my producer, Hend, arrived—or "Mama Hend," as I would later call her. Make no mistake, she was actually ten years younger than me. The reason I called her that was because she was like a mother to the team we assembled. She was short, with long black hair that reached to her waist—a kind of Egyptian Pocahontas. She had been on maternity leave for two years but was eager to get back to work. Given how she was sick and tired of the same routine and how the Egyptian media were locked in the 1980s, I knew she was a good fit for my team. As well, Khalifa, my director, had worked with her before and said that she was the best producer around.

The first time we met, I could see that Hend didn't really think

I was TV material, which was the same impression Khalifa had when he started directing me. Actually, many were betting that this was the first and last season of TV for me. They thought I would burn out quickly. I mean, it isn't really a high vote of confidence when your first contract gets shortened from two years to one.

The first order of business was to come up with a name. We tried a lot of catchy titles, but ultimately I decided to call the show *Albernameg*, which simply means: The Show.

The name was purposefully mundane. I told my team that all of those TV shows with catchy names were of low quality and that they all produced the same shitty shit. So why not make satirizing the name of the show the first order of business? We didn't need a flashy name to distract the viewer; our content would do the real work. It's like how the Zuckerbergs and the Jobses of the tech business operate—they wear the same fucking shirt every day, disregard the haters, and focus on content.

Once we got the name out of the way, we had a bigger problem. I was no comedian with absolutely no experience in acting or standup comedy. Remember, only a couple of weeks before I was making videos in the same room I washed my underwear. So there we were, a team led by a cardiac surgeon, with a director and producer who really didn't see me surviving, all attempting to make a television show. It sounded just like what failures are made of . . .

DRESSED FOR SUCCESS

Even though we had no idea what to expect, my television program finally debuted.

Let's just say it did pretty well for itself. After the first month we came in second only to the most popular and expensive show the channel aired. I was brought in as a guest on talk shows, gave interviews, and began to see my face pop up on posters in the streets announcing my program. Politicians and influential figures in society were glad to come to the show to be interviewed. This wasn't a hastily put together YouTube webisode program anymore; it was a full half-hour show, with a variety of segments and guests. It wasn't quite my dream of *The Daily Show*, but we were getting closer to its essence. In appearance we had graduated from the shitty version of an eighties TV show in Egypt to a crappy American version of a bad eighties MTV show. In Egypt this was something new and refreshing.

But we were still a high-flying trapeze act over hungry crocodiles. Our Christian network owner still proved to be a liability, and every time I made fun of an Islamist politician, both Salafis and the Muslim Brotherhood accused me of being a Christian hit man. It was as if they thought Sawiris was behind the scenes, saying, *You wanna play rough. Okay. Say hello to my little friend . . . Bassem Youssef.*

I didn't think much about it until we decided to make an episode about how different political powers view democracy. I made fun of everyone, but I have to be honest: the Islamist clips were way funnier than the non-Islamists ones. We got ahold of a clip from an interview between a sheikh and an Islamist sympathizer anchor who opened with the line, "You have a great quote saying that democracy is filth and we as Muslims should be avoiding it."

The sheikh went on to argue that democracy leads to freedom and this is why liberals seek it out. He proffered that freedom devoid of religious control would inevitably lead to sexual freedom and orgies happening in the streets (which sounds like heaven on earth to me). But this was what democracy reeked of in Islamists' eyes: horny people having sex in public, women losing their virginity, and sinful liberals imbibing everywhere. Brings back those sweet, sweet memories of people having "complete sexual relations" in Tahrir Square, right?

The videos we were finding were really good, and we thought we had done a good job of organizing and editing them before putting them on-air. But then I received a call from the manager of the channel.

"Bassem, we need to talk." It sounded like he wanted to break up with me.

He told me he saw the episode and that it was very good and all, but that maybe we should reconsider airing it. This was the only time the channel interfered with my content. By this point I had made fun of the channel, of the owner, and of everything else and no one had objected. What was different now?

"You know that we've never stopped you from saying whatever you wanted, right?" he said. "But we are facing quite a sensitive situation."

"And what situation is that?" I asked.

"Well, Sawiris, the owner of the channel, has been receiving serious death threats. He has even sent his children away from Egypt."

The Islamists had upped their game. Banners were hung in the streets asking people to boycott Sawiris, his channels, and his entire telecommunications company. I thought it was merely propaganda, but it actually led to angry Muslims attacking some of his offices and telecommunications outlets in defense of their religion.

I ultimately had to agree to what the manager asked for and canceled an episode that was particularly harsh in its ridiculing of the Islamists.

I had a love-hate relationship with the Islamists, though. Despite the propaganda against me and the attacks coming from their media hawks, most Islamists I met were really quite nice. They followed my show and watched it regularly. They were still skeptical about many things. Why does he work for a Christian? Why is he so hard on Islamists? Does he pray five times a day? Boxers or briefs? I explained to them that the satire was nothing personal, and if you are someone who wants to hold public office, you should be able to accept criticism and sarcasm. But as this was a totally new approach to our culture, the conversation usually ended with them praying for Allah to show me the right path.

Another odd occurrence from the debut of my show was that I started to get invited to many political events. Being popular because of comedy made several political bodies seek me out for appearances at their meetings and rallies. Politicians, whether they liked me or not, wanted to associate themselves with my notability, if you can believe that. I was invited to speak and people would listen. Most of the time I had absolutely no idea what the hell I was talking about, but it was an easy job, really. Just mention the words *freedom* and *revolution* a lot and all the liberals will cheer for you. Do that with a couple of recycled jokes from your videos and you are gold!

I was invited to speak at a conference about my experience going from YouTube fame to television, and how to use the new media to convey political messages. There were representatives from all political parties in attendance. After my speech, I talked with some of the Islamist party representatives. Some were from the Muslim Brotherhood and others from the new Salafi party called Al Nour, or "the Light." We had a long, heated discussion about whether or not we should apply Sharia Law in Egypt.

"So give me a good reason why we should apply Sharia Law?" I questioned.

"Well, it is proven that countries who apply Sharia Law have the lowest crime rates," answered one Salafi.

Now this is one of those bullshit answers you get whenever you talk with an Islamist. They are like the same people in America who argue against gun control because #GunsSaveLives. Oh really? Tell me again how a weapon with the sole purpose of injuring or killing whoever is on the other side of it is a great lifesaver.

I responded that the lowest crime rates are in Finland, Sweden, and Singapore, and if they had up and chosen to apply Sharia Law, well, I surely hadn't heard a thing about it. I also reminded him that sexual harassment is highest in Afghanistan, Saudi Arabia, and Egypt.

He claimed that if we were to better apply Sharia Law and, for example, punish adulterers by whipping them, we would limit the presence of brothel houses.

"Really?" I responded. "Well, first of all, according to Sharia, the real one, you can't convict someone for adultery unless you have four witnesses observing the whole thing from start to finish. So, presumably, the Sharia police will receive an anonymous tip. Then they will quickly move in on the brothel house and politely knock on the door. When no one answers because they are too busy discussing whether or not to perform the beast with two backs, they'll have to kick the door down. Well, now there's an audience. This is as good a time as any to cheat on your wife. So they patiently wait for the four officers to gather around their bed and watch them get nasty from the best possible angle? It sounds like we might as well be filming pornography."

He and the other fellows couldn't come up with a counter-argument. For thousands of Islamists who saw my show, it was the first time they had to face an opposing logic. Dismantling their weak narrative was like removing a single playing card from beneath their house of holy lies. This is why closed communities such as the Islamists and the military were not big fans of openly discussing their beliefs and convictions. They were running on blind faith and obedience, instead of reason and logic. And this is why both of those camps came together to crush whatever liberal movement emerged from the revolution. What came next was a page out of the shock-and-awe playbook, ISIS edition.

WELCOME TO KANDAHAR

It was a hot summer in Cairo.

There's nothing really special about that line, as it is always hot as balls in Cairo. It just felt like a poetic way to open this chapter.

The Islamists had left the square months earlier and were now preparing for the first parliamentary election after the revolution. The non-Islamic political powers were also trying to shape up for the elections, with very little hope of winning after having that referendum (yes-versus-no vote) defeat stamped on their asses. Meanwhile, the army, the real power in the country, was operating through an interim government that watched *everyone*.

Then you had the people remaining in the square. Every day the streets were blocked because of sit-ins, and every Friday there were huge demonstrations. I can't even remember now why there were demonstrations and sit-ins, but they could've been for anything: police reform, minimum wages, or Rihanna canceling her tour in the Middle East. The economy was in bad shape and the traffic was only getting worse. The everyday citizen couldn't see why the protestors continued to block downtown Cairo and cause a

headache for everyone around them. They started to see the protestors' causes as less and less important and began to correlate the
worsening economy and growing traffic with the revolution. The
"delinquents in Tahrir" was the new nickname bestowed on them.

It is fascinating to follow the trail of labels the protestors of
Tahrir Square were given—from "spies" to "heroes" to "revolutionaries" to "infidels" to "anarchists," and now "delinquents." It's not
too dissimilar from how the Occupy Wall Street protestors were
viewed in New York and across America. At first, many saw them
as "admirable activists" who were representative of the people, but
it didn't take long for the cause to fizzle out and for the remaining
protestors to be demoted to lazy nuisances who wanted free clothes
and food (and the opportunity to chant together!). The Arab Spring
was now a distant memory, and the promise of a new Egypt had
dematerialized, leaving only the same nightmarish life people had
always had.

There were attempts by the liberal forces to suggest and promote what they called "supra-constitution articles," which resem-
bled the American Bill of Rights; they wanted to introduce Egypt to
absolute equality, freedom, and all that other good stuff. You might
think this was something we'd all get down with, right? Ha! Both
the Islamists and the army were spooked by the idea of unchecked
liberty. How else could they control us without uniting behind that
common enemy of "freedom of thought"? A revolution liberates the
people from blind obedience, and those who want absolute control
are willing to use a tank or ancient scripture to achieve it. Power at
all costs.

The Islamists made a huge fuss about it. "How can something
be supra-constitutional?" they would say. "That implies it will be
held higher than Sharia Law." They argued that valuing absolute
equality and absolute rights over Sharia law meant that Sharia

would no longer matter. Uh-oh. That would lead to "liberal sinners" having all the freedom in the world to perform sex acts on benches, in bedrooms, under bridges, while riding bikes, or maybe while doing ballet or BASE jumping. Copulation would break out like the common cold and soon everyone would be sex zombies.

Days and weeks on end, the Islamists aired television campaigns that pounded against the supra-constitution articles.

"The 20 percent minority are trying to dictate what the Islamic majority should do," their ads would espouse. "And worst of all they want to abolish Sharia."

This thought process reminded me of what an outspoken sheikh named Shouman had said about the movie *Titanic*, which I mocked on my show. He said that the reason the *Titanic* sank was because Kate Winslet posed nude for Leonardo DiCaprio, essentially claiming that a fictional nude portrait session caused the wrath of God to doom the (actual) entire ship and its passengers to a watery grave. For this sheikh, if God did this to the *Titanic*, imagine what He could do to Egypt if it abandoned the rule of Sharia.

"Liberalism means that your mama would have to take off her hijab," he shouted in one of his sermons. This became the most famous Internet meme in Egypt. At a different rally he shouted, "When you die and you are in your grave being questioned by angels, you will be asked about your God and how you worshiped him, your religion and how you followed it, and Sharia Law and how you defended it. Thus, voting yes in the referendum is considered a holy war to defend God and his Sharia."

A call was made out to all "jealous Muslims" to defend their God by taking back Tahrir Square, to protect Sharia and the beloved army from infidels. "It is time to purify the square from those drug addicts and faggots," a prominent sheikh shouted to a crowd of Islamists before marching to Tahrir.

On that particular day of purification the square was filled with the Islamist leaders and their goons, ones that had never stepped foot in the place because they were told by the same sheikhs months earlier when the revolution was at its peak that participation of any kind in politics is haram. But now, all of a sudden, occupying the square was a holy mission from God. Countless buses shuttled people from villages and remote rural areas to Tahrir. Not all of them were Islamist activists: many were simple peasants and workers who were responding to the call to protect their religion.

We had never seen the square that packed. The revolutionary songs were replaced by jihadi chants, and the Egyptian flag shared the stage with flags from Saudi Arabia and al-Qaeda, in addition to photos of Bin Ladin. People watched on television with a mixture of disgust and horror: *Is this why we started the revolution?*

It was a pure power flex by the Islamists. The media sarcastically called it "Kandahar Friday," alluding to Afghanistan's second biggest city and its radical Islamic militants, the Taliban.

The amount of money used to mobilize all of these people was astonishing. The army seemed to turn a blind eye to the millions of dollars flown from Saudi Arabia to the Salafis. It was the same army that a couple of months earlier allowed more than three thousand jihadists to come back from Afghanistan, after more than twenty years of imposing a travel ban. It was the same army that would crack down on liberal human rights organizations that were funded through American aid, for a fraction of the money flooding in from Saudi Arabia (more on that to come).

The same thing was happening in Syria. Bashar al-Assad, their bloody dictator, released thousands of jihadists from jail once revolution erupted there. Later, these people became the leaders of ISIS. A peaceful revolution turned into a bloody Islamic jihad. The textbook of fear is the same everywhere.

That day in Tahrir, the Muslim Brotherhood didn't have the loudest voices, but they were definitely a part of the Islamist ranks. They despised the Salafis, but they reveled in the fact that they could exploit their numbers.

At night, the Islamic television anchors were having the holiest orgasms of their lives. They proved they could gather masses and show us, the infidels, that they were here to stay.

The "supra-constitution articles" were scratched, of course, and with them went all the articles that protected human rights and the ability to monitor the military budget. It was obvious who the winners were that day. The Islamists had performed their version of "shock and awe," the military received extended protection, and the revolution had lost its spark.

Tahrir Square was officially dead.

ISLAM IS COMING!

Salafis despise women. This is a fact. It is the same with fanatics of any religion all over the world. Salafis who cover women in black potato sacks are no different from what the extreme Hasidic Jews do to their women. Sex is an abomination unless one can have it with four teenage brides, or an altar boy in a Catholic church . . . then it's God's will!

As many parts of the world started to become more forward thinking about their treatment of women, many Arab countries appeared backward for their misogyny. So Egypt and its new parliamentary law made it mandatory for a party to put at least one woman on its ballot in each district. This was no problem for the Muslim Brotherhood, which was used to having women in their campaigns and were shrewd in using women to approach the housewives in poor areas and talk to them in order to get votes.

The real problem was with the Salafis. They come from the same school of thought as the Saudi Wahhabis, who consider women merely walking vaginas with nothing to do but receive sex and raise children. In their ideology, women should just stay at home, and if they do get out they should do so only from extreme necessity, like shopping for the latest Victoria's Secret collection to keep their husbands' boners alive.

Wahhabism is basically the most ultraconservative branch of Islam you can practice on this planet. Its practitioners are the ones who have banned women in Saudi Arabia from driving, which is not just an arbitrary decision based on blind faith and utmost stupidity. No, no, no! As a matter of fact, there are good scientific reasons for doing so, according to them—like the time a sheikh on a Saudi channel proved that women are not fit for driving because "modern science proves women who drive damage their uterus and Fallopian tubes." Interestingly enough, modern science also proves he's a dick.

Another so-called Saudi, a historian and social expert, went on Lebanese TV to give us a totally different angle on this problem. He said that the main reason women don't drive in Saudi Arabia is because cities are far apart. "What if the car breaks down and she gets raped on the highway?" he proposed.

The female Lebanese anchor retorted, "Well, women drive in the West, why is that not a concern?"

"For Western women rape is not a big deal," he answered.

"What?" the anchor asked in horror. "What do you mean it's not a big deal?"

"Well, in the West it is just a moral issue, but in Saudi Arabia it is a religious and social issue, it affects the whole community. Women in the West will just get over it. They don't have our complicated religious and social matrix."

The female anchor couldn't hold back her laughter. She asked, "Well, if the woman cannot drive because she would be raped, and the only way to get around is using a chauffeur, the chauffeur could still rape her, right?"

"That is why I have suggested something, but the authorities won't listen to me. Women should be accompanied by foreign female chauffeurs!"

In the Wahhabi and Salafi mentalities it is haram (like everything else in the world) for men to show photos of their women. Twenty years ago it was haram to take photos in general because "you should not replicate the creation of Allah." But since the TV star sheikhs hired professional photographers to give them professional photo shoots, they had to issue custom-made fatwas stating that it's okay for men to do so. But now with the new parliamentary mandate, how could they have female candidates' photos on the banners? And how could they urge millions of totally covered women who weren't allowed to leave the house to go vote?

To solve the first dilemma, they decided to put women in a black *niqab* for the picture, which really didn't make any sense because all you could see was a face with a black ninja-like cover over it. Then they thought of something even more brilliant: to put a photo of a flower instead of a photo of a human being next to the woman's name. Just like that.

Then came the biggest problem of all. How could they mobilize the masses of women that were previously told to stay at home and not leave unless necessary? How could they tell them to take part in elections while the political operation was viewed as an abomination from Satan?

The solution came in the form of women's conferences all over the country. Now, you would think that a women's conference would have some women speakers, right? Wrong! The left side of the audience were women all covered in black and the right side was filled with men. The women all sat quietly listening to male sheikhs deliver speeches on women's issues. The sheikhs emphasized that women were indeed lesser than men but that they were now needed more than ever to stand beside Islam. "It is true that we had restrictions on women going to vote and being part of the political process," one sheikh admitted, "but now it is different. There is a real danger against Islam and we should all use every possible measure to protect it. Necessities allow for trespasses." Which is the Islamic way of saying the end justifies the means.

Every political party had television commercials for their campaigns. Even the Muslim Brotherhood had tried to feign balanced ads, with some women wearing the hijab and others not. However, the Salafi Al Nour party had commercials of a guy with a long beard explaining to a female why choosing Al Nour is the best option; that female was only seven years old. If she was any older than that, it would have been required to pixelate her face. I'm still not sure why they didn't just have the bearded man talking to a pretty flower. It would've been the start of a good hallucination scene in a cheesy independent movie.

Another common thread on the Islamists' channels was the new slogan by many Salafis, "Islam is coming!" *Where did it go in the first place?*

In a country where more than 90 percent are Muslims and 90 percent of women are covered and mosques are more abundant that Walmarts in the States, I can assure you Islam has never left. The Brotherhood had a less hysterical, subtler message than the Salafis. They just resurrected their slogan "Islam is the solution." *We just have to be closer to God and everything will be all right!* Both of them were calling to make Egypt "Islamic again." Sound familiar?

One day I went to my hairdresser for a cut, in addition to wanting to survey the blue-collar working-class people who were his customers. "Why would you vote for the Islamists?" I asked them, telling them that mixing religion and politics was very dangerous. After a lot of bullshit excuses, one guy gave me an honest answer—not necessarily logical, but honest: "Sir, we are people entrenched in sin. We smoke, do drugs, drink alcohol, we commit all sorts of sins. We need this country to be better, and God will not allow this if we have all those sins. So maybe those pious people will lead us to become better Muslims, and God will be happier with us."

That logic blew my mind. So basically he was repenting for his sins by electing someone who would not just represent him in the parliament but who would represent him in heaven too! He continued to surprise me when he told me he had friends who worked as waiters in five-star hotels and coastal resorts who were not happy because they had to serve alcohol, since the consumption of it is forbidden in Islam. He told me that all of them were going to vote for the Muslim Brotherhood. People might vote for ideological reasons, emotional reasons, bullshit reasons, but only here in Egypt will people vote out of guilt.

Election Day came, and for the first time in history women dominated the scene. The Islamists' plan worked, and women came to defend their precious religion against whatever was out there to get it.

It was really no surprise when the results came out. It was another crushing defeat for the useless, good-for-nothing liberal camp. It didn't matter how much money they threw at their cause or how much effective campaigning they did, liberal and leftist parties were absolutely helpless. Egyptian politics was not a simple competition between ideologies; it was a competition against Allah himself.

It didn't matter what jokes I threw around on my program, either. Satire seemed an ineffective means to change people's minds. After I finished the filming of an episode days after the election, my driver took me back home. He had been driving me for a few months now, and on the way to and from work we had intense discussions about politics, in which I ceaselessly explained why it was dangerous to elect people hiding behind the cloth of religion. On our way home that night, I asked him whom he voted for. "Well, for the Muslim Brotherhood, sir," he said casually. "Let's pray to Allah to bestow his mercy on us and reward us for that good decision. After all, they are people of God."

Oh, fuck me!

THE HALAL
PARLIAMENT

With a 75 percent majority, we had a true Islamic parliament: 49
percent of the vote went to the Muslim Brotherhood and 26 percent
went to the Al Nour party of the Salafis. But, as far as the parliament
went, they were united. The Islamic channels were elated to talk
about this monumental victory for Islam.

On the first day of the parliament there is usually a tradition
of standing up for the national anthem. Many Salafis members did
not stand. And no, they did not stand to follow in the footsteps of
Colin Kaepernick or Black Lives Matter or for the well-being of the
oppressed and the abused. Their party leader put it this way: "It is
an abomination. We only stand for Allah. The national anthem is
a Western tradition. We should not abide by it." A couple of years
later this leader would be seen standing alongside the military as
the national anthem played. He would also sit, fetch, and roll over
whenever the military asked him to do so.

There is another tradition in which every parliament member
stands up and swears to protect the law and the constitution. It goes
like this: "I swear to protect, blah-blah, and maintain, blah-blah-
blah, the law, blah, country, blah, and the constitution."

But for the first time in history we heard it with some addi-
tional malarkey. Each Islamic member stood up, recited the pledge

as is, and then added "to maintain and protect and obey the constitution in a way that does not contradict with the Sharia of Allah."

This made many people furious. It wasn't that they tampered with the pledge, it was the fact that they showed their intention to interpret the law of the land through the lens of Sharia, and that religion would trump everything else.

For my show, though, this was the joke that kept on giving. We would all jokingly swear to not drink alcohol, commit adultery, steal, or cheat "in a way that doesn't contradict with the Sharia of Allah." As long as you said those magic words, all bad behavior could be absolved. Underneath the jokes and smart punch lines, however, many people in my circle were scared.

We are an interesting society. We might be religious, but we are also class conscious, and the "classy" educated circles were basically reacting to the parliament sessions like the Armageddon apocalypse.

I used to go to a nice sports club called Gezira Club, one of those hard-to-get-in country clubs. This is where you will find people from the upper class of society and an abundance of high-class "has-beens" that might have lost their wealth but not their arrogance. An integral part of their character was the cynicism and the innate hate they had for the younger generation for the simple fact that the young presumably had more time left to live on earth. The most interesting members were the old women whose faces stopped giving a fuck and just faltered under the years of plastic surgery.

These people at the club gathered to watch the parliament sessions with utmost disgust. They despised the fact that those fanatic zealots who came from rural areas and had absolutely no credentials other than a beard and backward dogmatic ideology were now the face of the first elected parliament. A lot of these older people blamed the younger people for the revolution, and, subsequently, the new government that came with it. This is the result of *your revolution*, they would shout in our faces.

In the first week of parliamentary sessions, a well-known Islamic fanatic stood up in the middle of the session and started to recite the call to prayer. The president of the parliament was from the Muslim Brotherhood and scolded the man.

"How could you prevent me from calling for holy prayer?" the man asked the president. "Aren't you a Muslim?"

"I am more Muslim than you are, but this is not the time or the place," the head of parliament answered.

No one would remember anything from that session other than that argument between a right-wing Islamist and an even further right-wing Islamist, so I dedicated a big chunk of my show to it. I wanted to show people that there is not just one version of Islam. And if Muslim Brotherhood leadership was not religious enough by Salafi standards, then what would that make the rest of us?

The parliament sessions were long and boring, but we were the only ones who had a dedicated team to record and report on everything happening there. We were like the Egyptian version of C-Span.

There were only a handful of liberal representatives in the middle of this parliamentary madness. Every time one of them spoke he was heckled and interrupted like a bad standup comedian performing for a tough crowd. There were no real discussions; the Islamists were driven like herds to the sessions to approve what was already pre-dictated by their leaders. It seemed a tight pact until the scandals started flooding in.

ONLY GOD "NOSE"
(OR HOW I BLEW MY SALAFI NOSE OFF)

One of the really haram things in Islam is plastic surgery. If that is the body and face given to you, you should not interfere with God's creation. This is very bad news for the silicone business if a true caliphate is ever established, or if that fatwa resonated around the world, it would be a disaster. I mean, one of the main reasons I watched the American show *Two and a Half Men* was for the endless stock of surgically enhanced women who appeared in it. (Another sentence planted by my editor, such a sexist, horrible man.)

So what is the connection among plastic surgery, Salafi fatwas, and parliament members? Well, one of them went under the knife—and lied about it!

The Salafi Al Nour party issued a statement about one of its parliament leaders, El Belkeemy, being "attacked and mugged" while driving his car on a highway. There were pictures of him in the hospital with his face halfway bandaged. He talked to the press, giving details of the incident, saying that gang members beat him badly and took a bag of money that belonged to his business. The idea of carrying large sums of money in a bag made it sound like he was in some wild, wild West movie. All the same, the religious Facebook pages and their media suggested that the attack was meant to scare the good people of the Al Nour party into thinking the assailants were enemies of the party (and of course of Islam). They really milked that for a few days.

Then it all came crumbling down.

A source in the hospital leaked documents that this was no injury resulting from an attack. It was plastic surgery for his nose. A *Salafi* just had a nose job. This is like people discovering that Donald Trump's biological mother was a Mexican illegal immigrant who worked as a gay go-go dancer and never paid her federal taxes. (Oh wait, neither did Trump!)

What made it worse was that the prime minister and the party denied the claims by the hospital and said it was all a cheap way to tarnish the Islamists' image. When Belkeemy finally came clean, he kind of half-assed it. He said he had to do the surgery because he had a life-threatening case of sleep apnea, which again the hospital promptly refuted. The clips we used about this scandal were, needless to say, priceless. Normal people began to see that a beard was not synonymous with honesty. It was simply a patchy place to hide one's lies.

To be fair, the party fired Belkeemy and said that he was not representative of the values and morals that they stood for. It was a good political move and good damage control. But the damage had already been done. And it didn't help when a few weeks later another one of their party was caught in the middle of an "indecent act" with a woman in his car.

These stories might sound insignificant but they are telling of the nature of these political Islam hawks, who are no different from many priests, senators, or other vocal right-wing uber-conservative personalities who use religion and tradition to win over the people and then end up caught in a sex scandal. I am looking at you, Jimmy Swaggart! (Insert crying, sweaty-face meme here.)

Aside from the jokes their gaffes provided for our show, this Islamic parliament seemed up to the important task of getting rid of something that seemed quite dispensable. The very thing that had got them there . . . the revolution.

A LEAGUE OF EXTRAORDINARY JERKS

The parliament was not just about nose jobs and stupid gaffes. This was supposedly the "revolution parliament." The one that came after a revolution by the free will of the people. However, those people who had risen to power because of the revolution did their best to betray it every day on the job. To explain this better, let me take you back a few months to before that parliament was elected.

When Mubarak stepped down, everyone danced and cheered and thought that the revolution was over. That couldn't be further from the truth. It's not just the fact that the military and their Islamist surrogates were covertly bringing back the old regime one way or another, it was also the fact that many of the families of the young people who were killed or injured during the protests were totally ignored. No medical compensation was given, nor was there recognition of their sacrifices, which made it possible for the new regime to have their power in the first place.

The families of those injured, killed, or just plain shamed decided to have a sit-in at Tahrir Square that continued for months, all the way up to November of the same year, 2011, when the parliamentary elections commenced.

On a mild November night, security forces swarmed the square and attacked and arrested members of those families. Everyone was furious, and thousands of protestors fled back to the square, leading to the bloodiest clashes since the revolution had ended. Dozens were killed and many more were injured.

As the people were killed in the square, the Islamic media and even many of the state-run media were further attacking the protestors, insinuating that they were deliberately sabotaging the parliamentary elections. What was interesting was that the Islamists, who benefited from the revolution, used the same exact negative propaganda that was used against it only a few months earlier—mainly that the protestors were "paid operatives" aiming to sabotage the country.

Yet again, Tahrir Square was shut down due to the clashes. Not a single camera covered what was actually going on within the square. Many television crews were kicked out because of how the protestors saw these channels manipulating the truth about them.

We decided we had to broadcast from inside the square à la *The Daily Show* and find a way to satirically report the situation. The problem was, we had never tried something like that before and didn't have a regular team of correspondents like Samantha Bee or John Oliver. Also, there was a major safety concern that the crew would be subjected to a great deal of danger if they were caught between the clashes.

So I made an executive decision and decided to go and cover it myself. My team objected because they thought it too dangerous. In the end a very limited crew accompanied me.

"I love you as a brother," Tarek told me. "But for absolutely selfish reasons I can't let you go; if something happened to you our investment will be doomed," he added jokingly.

I appreciated the fact that I was a commodity worth protecting, but my mind was set. I knew many of the protestors personally and I saw how unfairly they were being treated in the media.

I couldn't tell my wife or my overly concerned mother about this as it would just add an extra unnecessary burden. As a matter of fact, while I was in the square, I had to run away from the clashes every time my mom called my cell phone to pretend to be in the office. That's right, we are more afraid of our Middle Eastern mothers than rubber bullets!

Tahrir Square was battered, the smell of gas so strong that I had to wear a mask even when I was more than half a mile away.

How could I make this scene light and sarcastic?

There were injured people who had to be carried on motorcycles all the way to makeshift clinics safely outside of the confrontation line.

Egypt never failed to amaze me. Here you have "the state" killing and maiming its citizens through its police force, while the same "state" sent an abundant number of ambulances from the ministry of health to treat injured protestors and transfer them to state-owned hospitals. The irony was too much.

As the cameraman and I advanced farther into the square, many people were hostile toward the camera, but when they recognized me they openly greeted us. My pro-revolution position gave me some street cred and a lot of needed protection for the crew.

What had I gotten myself into?

My field-reporting and stone-throwing skills were proven deficient earlier in the year. I didn't have a script or a plan. I asked stupid questions of people who were too nice and even too naive not to take me seriously. Still to this day, I don't know how I was not punched in the face.

Because Egypt is a class-conscious society, as previously mentioned, I was adamant about filming beautiful, classy people: young, vibrant boys and girls who were far from thugs, but who were also just normal humans who deserved to live a productive life. As if to say "not-so-nice-looking people" deserved to die. I hate the way this world operates, I truly do.

I interviewed doctors, protestors, volunteers, and spectators. People told me that the police had imported a new type of gas that could not be combated through the usual methods. Canisters with MADE IN THE USA stamped on them were given to me to show to the camera. Thanks, Obama?

I interviewed young Islamists who didn't agree with their opportunistic leaders and were there to support the protestors. I interviewed older, privileged ladies who were supposed to be at home cursing these people on the street, but instead chose to be there on their side.

This was the closest to the "spirit of the revolution" I had seen in months.

"Let's wrap it up, Bassem, we have enough footage," my producer told me.

But I was not satisfied. We were shooting only in the middle of the square, away from the confrontation line. I wanted to show the clashes from the front. My crew objected, but I insisted we go. "It's going to be fun," I said, laughing, but the truth is I was freaking terrified.

We advanced farther, and watched four people rush in the opposite direction carrying a kid younger than fifteen covering his left eye with blood gushing out. This kid, like many others, had lost an eye because of a rubber bullet. Khalifa, my director, looked at me as if to say, *Dude, we didn't sign up for this.*

I continued advancing but then stopped. The smell of gas was horrible and I was almost blinded by it. The cameraman, the director, and the producers were all tearing up and couldn't handle the smell anymore.

When we got back to safety, I owned up to the camera about how much of a pussy I was for not withstanding a few minutes of smelling gas while these people had been fighting through it for days.

I wanted to reconnect with the people in the square. I wanted to show how the Muslim Brotherhood had bailed on us, all of us, but I was afraid. The popularity of the Brotherhood was massive going into the elections. And again I had this curse of appearing to be a puppet of a Christian billionaire.

So we decided to write a rap song for the episode, dissing the Brotherhood, showing how they had always bailed on us in order to appease authority.

This episode and the song were great hits. If we had such a thing as an Egyptian *Billboard* the song would have made it to the top of the charts. People from all walks of life were worked up over the song like I'd never seen before, and were playing it in their cars and in the nightclubs. It was monumental because we showed how the old regime, the state-run media, the Islamist media, the Islamist parties, and the repressive police all sided together to work against whatever remained of the revolution.

But only a few weeks after the Brotherhood got into the parliament, new clashes with security forces erupted downtown. More people were killed and many more were injured. I know this sounds repetitive, but try walking in our shoes for a month. It is even more depressing.

The liberal minority in the parliament demanded an investigation and reported that police brutality, which incited the revolution to erupt in the first place, hadn't changed a bit since the revolution.

The Islamist members, the same ones who had suffered police brutality and persecution over the years, heckled those who spoke against police brutality. One member after another stood up to praise the minister of interior and accuse those "thugs" in the streets of trying to destabilize the country. Another Islamist member announced that he had "evidence" that all the protestors were on drugs and were paid money to disrupt the peace.

Then came a real whopper of an announcement from the head of parliament: "The minister of interior told me that no shots were fired and that riot police forces don't even carry shots with them."

Then who the fuck was shooting at us a few weeks earlier, the guys from *Duck Dynasty*?

The majority clapped and cheered as if their team had scored a touchdown. Then one of the non-Islamist members stood up and announced that he had gone to investigate the scene of the clashes and had found bullet casings on the ground, which instantly proved the minister was lying. He held the bullets in his hand for the entire parliament and cameras to see.

That scene was priceless. The Islamist members around him converged on the poor guy and tried to snatch the bullets from his hand, as if they had seen their parents having sex and wanted to unsee this horrific image.

The same people who had basically been fucked by the state for decades had now become whips for the state. In eighteen months' time, many of those Islamist members would either be jailed or killed in the streets by the same minister they were protecting. And that parliament member who stood with the bullets in his hand? He would be on every television screen justifying the need to kill them.

One day you're down, the next you're up. Life's really a bitch, huh?

GIVE US YOUR MONEY AND GET THE HELL OUT

As an Egyptian citizen, I have no idea how I should feel about America. On a daily basis outside the American embassy you can find lines for visas longer than the ones outside of Best Buy on Black Friday. The cinemas in my country are full of American movies. The television channels are loaded with American sitcoms. Every time an Egyptian president visits America, the state-run media cover the visits with more attention than TMZ would do for another Kardashian wedding. When Barack Obama visited Egypt in 2009, everyone was charmed by his "Al salamo alikom" greetings and were elated that Obama might have actually owned up and returned to his Muslim roots. A headline in one of the biggest Egyptian newspapers announced that Obama enjoyed his Egyptian breakfast and fell in love with our falafel. With all the money the American government funnels into our military, the least we could do was give him a good meal.

We receive $1.3 billion in military aid each year from America, plus more money to "support democracy." Big mistake! In order for Egypt to get the $1.3 billion in deadly weapons, we needed to appear as if we were financially supporting free speech and democratic organizations. In turn, these outspoken organizations would come right back and object to the American money used to grow the military. It was a vicious, vicious cycle.

A big chunk of that money to support democracy went to human rights organizations and institutions to train individuals in different aspects of the democratic process: how to manage candidates and voters, and even how to organize your potluck events. For years, the American government had been financing these activities right there under the nose of Mubarak, the army, and intelligence agencies.

And then one day, in a beautifully orchestrated manner, the state-run media and Islamist media decided that Egypt wasn't going to support those organizations anymore. Weird characters started becoming regular guests on television shows, and they talked about their experiences with these "shady" organizations. A short, fat guy who looked exactly like Megamind (even I have seen that movie), minus the blue skin, came on many TV shows to expose the "American plot against Egypt." This guy gave more or less the same story each time but tweaked it according to each show's audience. For Islamic channels he would emphasize the grave danger these organizations posed to Islam, while for state-run media he'd explain how America was conspiring against the Egyptian army. You know—that same army that willingly accepted $1.3 billion each year from the U.S. He would show his membership cards for these organizations and say, "There is no honor for me to stay a part of these heinous establishments," before ripping them up. He did that on four different shows. How many membership cards did this guy have? And if he tore up all of his membership cards how was he going to get his tenth smoothie for free?

This guy is what we call in Arabic *amnagy*, which is a derogatory term for being a dog to different branches of the secret police. There are many of these amnagy-type characters to be found—whether they are working for newspapers or television channels, or even as university faculty members. When needed, they will write articles or appear on television spouting whatever is dictated by the secret police.

Two of my dear friends were working in one of these organizations with Americans who were helping different political parties manage their elections. They called to tell me that the police and the Egyptian NSA had already cracked down on their headquarters and that they might be pressing charges.

Again I decided to go and expose this problem for what it really was while every other television program waged war on international human rights and American aid organizations. For the most part, I am not a fan of American aid. I personally think a lot of it is a big scam aimed to line the pockets of many American contractors. But the hysteria that was building just meant that everyone would be accused sooner or later of supporting human rights.

"Human rights" became an infamous phrase. In the state-run media, they accused anyone supporting human rights of using it as an excuse to create chaos to destroy the country from within. On religious channels, human rights were synonymous with unchecked freedom that would lead to every single person in the country having promiscuous sex or being gay or both! Oh brother, here we go again with the sex shaming!

Now, I should give my American readers some context here. Not since the French came to your aid during the Revolutionary War have you had an entire country assist in fighting a common enemy on your soil. South Africans don't come tell you how to run your government elections. Japanese don't donate money to support your homeless. Norwegians don't call you out for your treatment of minorities. And Brazilians don't give you over a billion dollars to help you purchase tanks and fighter jets with the caveat that you'd better support free speech too. So it may be difficult for you to understand the mentality other countries have about America when it deals with the rest of the world's "human rights." There is a certain amount of suspicion about what kind of closed-door trade-off must be occurring for the aid to be provided. Considering America is the biggest supporter of Israel, which has fought four wars with Egypt, Egyptians can't help but throw some side-eye at your "good intentions." Now, we all know that a lot of people have been positively impacted by this kind of work, but our state-run media have twisted it into another reason we shouldn't trust the Western world.

So against the advice of my own team, I hosted a friend of mine who worked with Human Rights Watch on the program. They didn't want me being associated with an entity that was perceived as on its way down in society. However, it astounded me that many of the Islamists parties went to these organizations to get training in election management and campaigning. Many of those made it into the parliament *because* of the training they received.

As predicted by the earlier arrival of the amnagy, paid public service announcements by the state's intelligence agency suddenly started hitting the airwaves. They showed a foreign man sitting in a coffee shop among the locals. The camera showed his evil hawkish eyes scanning the perimeter for vulnerable Egyptians to extract information from. A close-up of his ear insinuated he was eavesdropping on their conversation. I don't know what kind of important information some foreigner would get from sitting in a local coffee shop, since Egyptian men usually go to these shops to get away from their wives, bitch about their wives, or brag about imaginary sexual adventures not involving their wives. In the PSA the alleged "spy" tries to get friendly with the locals and starts speaking in broken Arabic. The gullible Egyptians start to pour their souls out, supposedly giving him valuable information. Finally, a dude tells him something that is supposedly very important, and after hearing it he sits with a sinister smile on his face while saying in a horrible English accent, "Really?"

How they couldn't get a guy to pronounce that right is beyond me! It was one fucking word, people! The screen abruptly freezes and a voice-over states, "Every word has a price, a word can save a nation." This was kind of a throwback video version of the WWII posters warning you that "loose lips can cost lives."

This particular PSA caused the guy who played the foreign spy to get into some real trouble. He was actually a struggling Egyptian actor trying to make his way, when he was recognized at a coffee shop and drew suspicion from some locals. They actually beat this guy up, and he had to come out to the newspapers swearing he was a real, red-blooded Egyptian.

This backlash caused the Egyptian government to decide to shut down those American centers and detain many of their employees. My friends were among the detained.

All the media hailed the decision as a move to restore Egypt's sovereignty. Pundits came out on television declaring the end of American dominance and of American attempts to affect Egyptian political decisions. Media campaigns were launched to free Egypt from the "humiliating chains" of American aid. Celebrities and Islamic leaders were on magazine covers leading donation campaigns to collect money from Egyptians to compensate for American dollars. Officers vowed to punish all the American operatives who had played parts in sabotaging Egypt from the inside. Photos of them standing trial were all over the news.

Then out of nowhere, all the Americans who were on a no-fly list were driven to the airport in the middle of the night and sent back home; the army moved in on the various organizations and NGOs for some cheap local publicity, but eventually let those "spies and operatives" go because you can't really piss on your sugar daddy when he's giving you $1.3 billion every year.

After collecting millions from the pockets of hardworking Egyptians, the donation campaign disappeared as fast as it appeared. To this day, no one knows where the money went.

A GOOD CHRISTIAN DOESN'T REVOLT

To many fanatics in our country, Christians are seen as the secret ingredient in every conspiracy being cooked against Islam.

We weren't always like this. In the 1940s, before the military coup of Nasser, Egypt was one of the most diverse nations in the region, a true melting pot of religions and ethnicities, but something happened along the line. Was it the huge infusion of Saudi money into Egypt? Or maybe it was when military authorities thought it easier to use religion to mass-control people with shitty lives? What's better than looking forward to a second life with a heaven full of booze and women, both of which you can't get in your current life? Or maybe it is the very nature of military rule: they hate diversity and they don't know how to deal with it, so the best thing is to make everyone as homogeneous as the uniforms in their training camps.

The truth is, we pretend to be tolerant until we are really not.

Life was not that fair for Christians even before the Islamists acquired majority rule in the parliament. Under Mubarak they had their own share of inequality, which included official unequal representation in the government and not being able to build their own churches without going through a convoluted mess of bureaucratic red tape.

It was normal for Christians to hear hateful speeches against them during Friday prayer sermons blasted through the microphones from mosques near their homes. The Wahhabi sheikhs indoctrinated generations with myths about Christians, ranging from what they put in their food to how they fornicate. Discrimination against Christians is a common practice across the Arab and Islamic worlds, and to some extent is not necessarily a religious thing. It is more of an authority thing. You see, the more open and inclusive a society is, the more free and expressive their citizens. An authoritarian regime, whether military or religious, doesn't want diversity. Having masses of people who think the same, talk the same, and hate the same is much easier for maintaining control.

So when Muslims worry about Trump becoming president and how he will deal with Muslims, they are just worried they will be treated the same way they treat non-Muslims in their countries. Like shit.

Again, like Muslims in America, Egyptian Christians are told from a very young age to keep to themselves. Even their grand priests have that mind-set of avoiding anything that might piss off the government. But after the revolution many people changed, and many of the Christian youth became more involved in politics and protests.

In October 2011, Christians took to the streets on their own, which is stupid if you are a Christian living in Egypt. They were out to demand more equality and better political reform. It was a huge, peaceful march, the first of its kind in Egypt.

It was also the last.

After their long march the Christians stopped and assembled around the state television building. In the Arab world television buildings are even more secure than the presidential palace. This dates to a long tradition in which Arab coups could simply take control of the television and radio stations, announcing the new leader as president, and people could go on with their merry lives.

On that day twenty-six Christians were killed by the army's soldiers and tanks.

The tragedy was not limited to the huge death toll. Another tragedy was in how the media covered it. "Copts were attacking military units," said the anchor on the state-run television news. "We implore the *honorable citizens* to protect its army against the vile attack."

But this was actually a turning point in the course of the revolution, both because the death toll at this march was the largest number of civilians to die in one day since the beginning of the revolution and because the killing took place in front of the cameras and at the hands of the ruling authorities. Unfortunately, from here on out, death turned into a daily statistic. A week after this incident I was interviewed by a reporter who asked me what I thought about what had happened. I told him that an entire revolution had erupted because one kid was tortured to death in a police station. One death. Now death had become very easy to swallow. What was a couple more? When the military turned people into discarded commodities, there was no telling how high the death toll could climb.

SEVERAL WEEKS AFTER THIS INCIDENT, SEVENTY-FOUR FOOTBALL fans were killed during a riot at a football game. This appeared to be premeditated murder, chaos initiated by unknown thugs while the fans were caged in and left to die.

There were many speculations about how and why it happened. One theory was that the fans of this club (Al Ahly, the biggest club in Egypt and Africa) were the most vocal against authority. They chanted against police in their matches and had an active part in the demonstrations against the police and army.

The true explanation still remains a mystery, but the way the police managed the crisis, the fact that "shady" known criminals were allowed into the stadium, and how the fans were trapped there and left to die hardly made it appear like a "normal" sports riot. Nothing was adding up.

I didn't comprehend the magnitude of the tragedy until the next day when I looked outside the window of my office. Right across from our building stood one of the biggest mosques in Cairo with more than three thousand people standing outside it. These were the friends and family of some of the deceased waiting for the bodies to come out after the funeral prayers.

I found myself going downstairs and walking toward the crowd. As I was in the middle of it, deafening silence overcame me. This felt like a scene from a black-and-white avant-garde French movie where everything was in slow motion. One kid raised his head and recognized me, then another and another. No one rushed to ask me for a photo or a selfie as per usual. One man silently walked toward me and put his hand on my shoulder. "We need you to avenge us," he said somberly. "You are the only one that speaks in our voice."

I had no idea what to do. I was a satirist, for crying out loud, and now I was called upon for help? What had I gotten myself into?

The sad thing was, this was not the last horrific incident that made satire and laughter inappropriate. For the next couple of years, I was repeatedly called insensitive and rude for trying to make people laugh while there was blood in the streets.

When we broadcast the following week, people were still in mourning and none of the media outlets rose to the occasion. I decided to change my attire. Instead of wearing a suit I wore a black T-shirt that was designed for the victims of the football game massacre. We aired the episode in black-and-white and featured a video by the minister of defense at that time, who instead of accepting responsibility went out and insinuated that there were evil agents against the "Egyptian people." The same way Trump insinuated that the "Second Amendment people" could consider assassinating Hillary Clinton, the minister of defense asked the "honorable Egyptians" to go after activists and "traitors living amongst us." I mocked his comments and even used a logo that said "Lying Soldiers," which became popular after all the atrocities committed by the army. By using this logo I was basically putting the blame on the military, who were hiding behind an interim government. They were the ones running the show. They were the ones who killed the Christians directly, they were the ones who killed the football fans, and they took on the people in Tahrir Square indirectly through the police.

This episode stirred huge controversy. My mom called me screaming, "How dare you call them liars!"

"Mom, I didn't say that," I replied.

"I am not stupid, you used the logo," she answered.

"Well, I—"

"The army is the only standing institution in this country. We would be lost without it. Show some respect."

She'd already had a fight with me because I had indirectly attacked the army a few weeks earlier when they crushed the Christians under their tanks. My mom believed the army's story that the soldiers were defending themselves against those "Christian criminals." To my mom and her generation, the army could do no wrong.

And that was the core of the problem. The army was indeed much more sacred than religion, and was not allowed to be slandered in any way. Islam might have entered Egypt fifteen hundred years ago, but for seven thousand years before that Egypt was owned by an army.

BRA AND THE CITY

Despite the fact that almost a year had passed since the revolution ended, sit-ins in the streets of Cairo were as ubiquitous as Starbucks. It didn't matter that they became counterproductive; they were symbolic of the frustration that hadn't ceased since the revolution began. *Well, we thought we removed a regime once, why not do it again the same exact way?*

So our days went like this: demonstrations ending in sit-ins, days and days of blocked streets, and, occasionally, a violent confrontation that would trigger a complete blowup.

This time the trigger came in the form of a protestor at a sit-in who was kidnapped by the soldiers standing guard around the cabinet building. He was beaten up so badly, he nearly died. The next thing you know there was another shit-fan roller coaster. Now it was not just people versus security forces but a direct confrontation with the army forces. This time, they were not a Christian minority, either. They were people known to be in the square from day one. It would be hard to use sectarian excuses here.

It started the usual way. Angry protestors threw stones and some Molotov cocktails. Then the army forces used rubber bullets, real bullets, and tear gas, which was "normal" for them. But then the scene turned surreal. A bunch of soldiers stood on top of the cabinet building and threw chairs, drawers, unidentified pieces of furniture, and toilet seats. And to complete the picture, one soldier lowered his zipper and started urinating on the protestors. All we needed were some exposed boobs and a dragon, and we'd be on the set of a live taping of *Game of Thrones*.

Whereas the army used to try and apologize or cover up events, they didn't care anymore. What made the clash even worse was when more people joined the protests, many of them young women.

A young woman who wore a long black traditional dress and covered her head and face was struck and dragged to the ground. A couple of soldiers pulled back her dress while she was unconscious, and her body was exposed, revealing her underwear. One of the soldiers stomped on her, driving his military boot into her stomach. Every TV channel caught this on tape.

But, as I'm sure you've already guessed, the scumbags in the media rushed to the defense of the army. First they proclaimed that this was a computer-generated image, a photoshopped scene. They even got movie experts to say that the international television stations had hired experts to fool the Egyptian people and make them turn against their beloved army. When that didn't work, they did what a good right-wing asshole would do: they blamed the assault on what the young woman was wearing. "She was wearing nothing under that black dress but a blue bra. Who does that?" they cried. Before you knew it, the official story was that she was planted in the scene to "embarrass the army."

Sure, the American standard for going easy on a rapist is checking if he is a white swimmer, but in Egypt all you needed was a military uniform to get a free pass.

Society bought into it. The misogynist, sexist society in its ugliest form materialized through these sorry excuses for human beings.

The young woman was known as the "woman with the blue bra." No one ever saw her face, knew her name, or understood what happened to her after this incident.

I went into my office that day and told my team I would write this episode alone. You would think I had a lot of material to go on, and I did. But every time I played the videos where they were talking about the young woman, I broke down in tears. She might have been assaulted by the soldiers just once, but she was violated again and again by Egyptian television networks. I was fighting my tears while writing the script. I can't remember if what I was writing was funny or not, but I remember that I wanted to go after all those assholes with a vengeance. I got hold of a video from one of the most watched religious channels that showed the scumbags making fun of her. As we re-aired it I pretended to eat sunflower seeds and spit the shells out as I watched their hate speech. It gave the message that I was literally spitting on the "holy sheikhs" and their behavior. In the Arab world this is a major insult to direct at a religious authority. And for once I didn't care. I was proud of my defiance.

This episode earned the hate of both Islamists and blind military supporters. Luckily, at that time, the military was quickly losing points because of the repeated violence, arrests, and transgressions against the young people who once led the revolution, and because of the country's worsening economy. So the real attack came from the Islamists. They got private photos of me on the beach with my female friends, dancing the tango (yeah, I dance tango too, what about it?), and posted them on social media. They were trying to portray me as a deranged, dancing, half-naked, anti-Islamic dog. They didn't stop at anything, including openly praying for me and my family's destruction.

Every member in my household was harassed, their private lives splattered all over their screens (thankfully my nude photos weren't hacked into, like poor Jennifer Lawrence's, and included in the famous Fappening scandal of 2014).

My life had already been turned upside down, but I couldn't foresee what was to come: my contract was about to end, I was about to ask for the most ridiculous thing in the history of Arab television, I was about to meet my hero, and I was about to find myself in the middle of the biggest attack on the American embassy in Cairo. Fun times ahead!

AN IMPOSSIBLE PROPOSAL

Albernameg reached the end of the first season as the highest-rated program on the ONTV channel. The channel now regretted only signing the show to one season. We had to negotiate the second season from scratch. Sucked to be them!

The channel execs wanted to negotiate a longer contract, but by this time I had other dreams in mind. I didn't just want to do a pre-recorded program in an empty studio anymore. I wanted to go live.

"I want a theater with a live audience," I told them.

They didn't expect that because until then, such programming was totally unheard of in Egyptian television. Years of socialism and government control hadn't pushed people to be very creative, and like I said before, media were stuck in the 1980s.

However, things were slowly changing in the Middle East. The rich Saudi channels had started to buy the expensive *American Idol*, *The Voice*, *Got Talent*, and *The X Factor* franchises. The idea of having a local, small-size program that started out on the Internet to face those behemoth franchises was insane.

The station asked us for the expected budget and logistics, and we came up with a budget that was eight times what was spent on any other show. The channel thought we were delusional. Actually, every single person in the industry thought we were out of our minds.

Besides their balking at the money, the idea of bringing in a live audience was alien to the Arab world. People in charge of the industry didn't want to worry about audience reaction. They would just bring in two hundred warm bodies to cheer and clap for stupid content and then pay them with a little money and a hot meal. I refused to be part of a fake program where everyone applauds, even if you do a shitty job.

I remember while I was recruiting writers one candidate asked me, "So are you really going to get a real audience?"

"Yes, definitely," I answered.

"You are not going to use applause signs or have a dude cue them when to laugh?"

"No, that would be fake, we will have real laughter," I said.

"But what if they don't laugh?"

"Well, I guess we should just write better jokes."

He was too scared to come on board.

When we finally got an offer for our show it was from a new channel, CBC, that had been around for only a year. There were many questions surrounding this channel: they were spending a shit-ton of money and in no time were a top-rated channel; the owner supposedly made his money working in Kuwait, but he came from nowhere in the media world. There were other rumors that the channel's money came from certain "authorities" in the government, and whenever the word *authorities* is mentioned, it means the intelligence service, which had many of the old faces of the old media who supported Mubarak in its pocket, as well as many of the respected revolutionary faces sugarcoating CBC's image.

When we first got an offer from them to sit down and speak, I was hesitant. But they were the only channel in the market willing to entertain the idea of financing the show.

I told them straightaway that I would not accept any interference in the content, and that the moment they tried to interfere I'd walk away. I was worried about their agenda and it seemed that they were worried about mine.

"My job is to be a watchdog on media and authority," I told them. "I will make fun of whoever is going to be in power. The Islamists came to power and I will be against them head-on, the same for anyone else."

They were extremely shaky when I said that; everyone wanted to play nice since the Brotherhood was gaining more power in the country.

The negotiations were tough and Tarek, I, and the rest of the original production team of *Abernameg* ended up having to borrow money to pay for the deficit in the budget. They needed to see if the show was a success or not before they committed completely. We were thinking big, even though none of us had any experience or knew if this half-baked experiment was going to work.

One man knew how it worked. I had to go to him.

ENTER THE STEWART

Since those early days when I made videos in the laundry room in my apartment, I playfully imagined being a guest on Jon Stewart's show. I just didn't know how I would ever get there.

Within three weeks of starting my online show I had offers to speak to the local media. But by the fourth week some journalist from the *Daily Beast* wanted to interview me. It was the first time I talked to a foreign journalist about my work. I was excited, and I had one goal in mind: *Stewart has to read this. He has to find out what I'm attempting to do.*

So in the interview I simply inserted Jon Stewart's name in every other sentence: "Who was your inspiration?" . . . "Jon Stewart" . . . "What is your biggest dream?" . . . "To have a show like Jon Stewart's" . . . "How often do you have bowel movements?" . . . "Well, three times a day after watching reruns of *The Daily Show* with Jon Stewart."

My little subliminal trick worked and the first English article ever written about me was titled "Jon Stewart of the Nile." Heck! I added some Middle Eastern flavor to the man!

It wasn't long before more foreign news agencies were asking for interviews. I continued with the same strategy of dropping Jon Stewart's name in every single interview, until, one day, it worked!

After a year and a half I was interviewed by someone who was the ex-girlfriend of a senior writer and producer on *The Daily Show*.

This was in the summer of 2012, when my contract had just ended and we were having trouble getting the money for our crazy idea of a live audience show.

As I was going through the endless negotiations of our second season, I worked in the interim on a travel show called *America in Arabic*. It was a reality show about Arabs who live in America—basically *Keeping up with the Kardashians* without the boobs, gossip, breakups, drama, and someone's father turning into a woman. Instead it was thoughtful, objective, and *very* boring.

One of the cities we shot in was New York. I got ahold of that *Daily Show* producer and asked him if I could shadow the team to understand how they put together their show. He was amazingly helpful and actually invited me to come to the writers' room and the production meetings in addition to getting a good look at the stage. He even allowed me to shoot inside their building and include it as a part of my reality show.

This might have been the coolest day in my life. I was inside the freaking *Daily Show* and geeking out hard.

The most I had hoped for that day was to get a selfie with Jon Stewart and make it my Facebook profile picture. But shit just kept getting better and better . . . Jon Stewart invited me into his office for a chat.

I went in expecting it to last for maybe ten minutes, but it went on for an hour. We talked about the Middle East, world religions, politics, and how it's difficult to potty-train toddlers. When we compared the politics of hate and xenophobia in both of our countries we found things to be sadly similar. I discovered that I wasn't actually imitating him on my show; it was the same stupidity in both nations that was encouraging similar forms of satire. We were merely seizing the moment. I told him about my plans to have a theater, a live show, and that one day I would pay back the favor of his talking to me by inviting him as a guest on my show. Then I squealed like a fan girl after he shook my hand good-bye, and told him that I would never wash my hand again (I kid, I kid).

I WENT BACK TO MY *AMERICA IN ARABIC* TEAM AND LOOKED EM-barrassingly happy. My day was made, I couldn't ask for anything more. And yet, "more" was asked of me; Jon's assistant came looking for me to invite me to *be* on the show!!!

One year earlier, when a journalist had asked me what I'd do if I ever met Jon, I replied that I would try to impress him so completely that he would bring me on as a guest. Well, apparently it worked!

I came on his show and managed to hold my ground while not messing up. I got a few laughs from the audience too. I did it!

Later in the green room, he met with me and said, "You are a natural. I know you might find this weird, and that you made a leap of faith switching your career to be a satirist, but you will soon discover that you are made for this. You are not just another guest, you are a friend and a colleague."

As I write this now, I'm watching the last episode of Jon's *Daily Show* on my DVR. I miss that man like crazy.

WELL . . . ISLAM CAME AFTER ALL

As I was living in my own utopian state of mind from meeting, bonding, and appearing with Jon Stewart—another utopia was in the making back home.

The summer of 2012 was the one in which Egypt would, for the first time in history, truly elect a president.

You might ask, *Well, didn't you guys have presidential elections before?*

And I would answer, *Sure, but it was* that *kind of election,* you know, the one where you already know who will win? It was Egypt's legacy to create pharaohs and vote for them for life, and the afterlife . . .

Egypt had always been occupied by someone else throughout its history. The pharaohs built the pyramids and thought, *Eh, we can't top that,* got bored, and just gave up. Which paved the way for the Greeks, the Persians, the Romans, the Muslims, then different sectarian factions of Muslims, all the way to the French, the Ottoman Empire, and of course the British Empire, to make their mark on Egypt.

In Egypt we were always told that our country is the graveyard of invaders, a slogan that was ingrained in our heads at a very early age. It is even written on big banners greeting tourists just in case they have second thoughts! We grew up thinking that our country is invincible and that no invader would succeed in overcoming it. But as we grew older and looked back to our history we realized that our country was indeed just a graveyard for all invaders who stayed long enough to die there and hand it over to yet another invader.

Until 2005, we didn't have elections. As mentioned before, we had referendums with yes-or-no votes where there was only one candidate. During Nasser, the results of these referendums were 99.5 percent yes. I kid you not. There was one human being who said no to Nasser. That was the reason he was split in half.

Across the Arab world the Nasser voting phenomenon spread. Military coups were the new trend. The Saddams, the Ghaddafis, and the Assads of the Arab world were all inspired by Egypt's 1952 "revolution" (wink, wink, nod, nod).

There is a famous joke that comes from Syria, while under the rule of their dictator Assad senior (father of the current president). It goes something like this: A Syrian immigrant in London heads to the Syrian embassy to vote in the presidential elections (not really, it was a referendum of yes or no to the president). He decides that this time he will finally say no to Assad. After he casts his vote and begins to head home, he is suddenly struck with terror over what he has done. He decides to quickly return to the embassy, ask the officers for forgiveness, and change his vote to yes. When he arrives, he pleads with the officers to hand his ballot back to him so he can correct his grave mistake. The head officer approaches him and states, "Well, luckily, we had already changed it for you; don't do that again!"

Since the military took over in 1952 presidential referendums in Egypt all ended in a yes vote, ranging from 99.5 percent to 99.99 percent. With percentages like that, a president could have won three consecutive races without even trying.

Getting a little cocky, Mubarak decided to have "real" elections in 2005, in which he allowed other candidates to run against him. Given this new appearance of choice it was obvious that Mubarak's popularity had taken a sharp dip. After decades of enjoying 99 percent of votes it was sad to see the guy winning by only 88 percent! If only his ego had taken an 11 percent drop too.

So in 2012, a year after Mubarak stepped down, we had what we could call a real presidential election. The Muslim Brotherhood a year earlier had said that for the sake of the revolution they would not put up a candidate. So of course when the elections came, for the sake of the revolution they pushed *two* candidates.

The first candidate was Khairat al-Shater, a real strongman of the Muslim Brotherhood. However, he was quickly rejected due to his prison history, not for his scatological surname. He was the brains, the money, and had all the Islamic swag. When he was rejected, Mohamed Morsi, a mere employee in the Brotherhood, was pushed to run. Everyone knew who really called the shots, though. Through the Brotherhood, al-Shater launched what was called the "Renaissance Project," a huge PR campaign that glorified their master plan for the future of Egypt.

At that time I was between seasons and was still negotiating the nitty-gritty terms with CBC. All I had back then to voice my opinions was my Twitter account. With 140 characters at a time I was driving the Brotherhood crazy, making fun of their every move. Through their newspapers and television channels they launched a full-on public attack against me.

That's why it seemed odd when out of nowhere I received an invitation to meet with Mr. al-Shater himself. His people told me that he wanted to speak to me about the Renaissance Project and give me better insight into what was going on. It was the same policy of "hear from us, not about us" that they had started their campaign with a year earlier.

Tarek's father organized the invite. Okay, remember Tarek? My friend who started the show with me on the Internet? Yeah, funny story, his father was a lifelong member of the Muslim Brotherhood. Ironic, right? Even Tarek's brother started working with them too because he believed their rhetoric. Tarek didn't buy into all of that and frequently had problems with his family. They really didn't like the fact that he was producing my show. Sound complicated? Well, imagine how their family dinners used to go.

So I went to meet al-Shater and found out that the head of Google Egypt was also invited. I figured out that this was a PR move to make the Brotherhood look better.

The meeting was held in their headquarters and lasted for two and a half hours, though the guy from Google and I got to talk only a total of fifteen minutes. That should give you some perspective on what the "conversation" was like.

Al-Shater told us how happy he was to meet us, and I joked about how his media was not nearly as happy as he was with me. He then went on for half an hour explaining that the Brotherhood didn't have the experience to work in an open media environment and that they needed all the help they could get, even if it was from outside the Brotherhood. *Hmmm, the strongman needs my help?*

He went on and on about the Renaissance Project and how they'd developed it and how they'd adopted it from other success stories in the world, such as Brazil, Turkey, and Singapore.

I doubt you're surprised, but I didn't give two shits about the project. Tyrants all over the world have amazing projects: it just depends which end of the project you're on. I was worried about that tsunami of dogma taking over the country. I was worried about Egypt turning into Afghanistan and the government using Sharia law to curb civil liberties. So in the couple of minutes' window I was allowed to speak, I told him, "What you have told me about your project could be considered a well-written essay full of lofty language that doesn't really mean anything. I want to know why you insist on using religion as part of your rhetoric."

He answered with the same cunning method that I have seen Islamists use everywhere. "Well, since it is a democracy, I am free to choose my method and you are free to choose yours. If you are a liberal or a socialist you can put forward your ideology, so why can't I put forth mine? We both lay our ideologies on the table and people can choose for themselves. Isn't that democracy?"

Sounds pretty smart, right? Well, that might work with some people. They can shut down television anchors with this argument. But seeing how they manipulated democracy with it, he wasn't fooling me.

When he tried to return to his useless explanation about the Renaissance Project, I stopped him.

"Hold on one second," I said. "What you have just said doesn't really make much sense. Islam, socialism, liberalism, capitalism, and any other *-ism* out there could be marketed freely among the people as ideologies. But this can only apply if you have a fair playground. I can't play a game of basketball with you when you don't even need to defend your twenty-foot-tall hoop and mine is only five feet and you can dunk every time. This is what political-religious ideologies do. They make it unfair for other people who don't share your ideology. Secularism, on the other hand, is a fair playground. Now, your *-ism* is a method of play, a plan of attack and defense, but it shouldn't change the parameters of the court or the rules of the game. We are in a country where Sharia Law is the main source of legislation. It is already unfair to use religion for a political win because the law is on your side. When I disagree with a liberal or a socialist, I can knock his theories and policies out the window. I can simply tell him that they are wrong by logically arguing my position. But how can you accept it when I tell you that you are wrong when you claim to be speaking in the name of God? I can't compete with God and I can't tell you that God is wrong. And as far as the people go, you know that we have a very high illiteracy rate and they will follow religion over reason every time."

Then I told him something that I couldn't have known would actually come true a year and a half later. "You are trying to present yourself as right-wing, and you think that in actuality you are only slightly right of center, but the truth is, you will be drawn further and further by the Salafis, which will lead to your radical downfall."

As I finished, the other men in the room were looking at each other, not used to seeing someone talking back to their feared leader. Another problem in our Arab world is that our old men are used to one-sided conversations, whether they are preaching at a sermon or in army camps. They love the sound of their own voices. That's why, despite the apparent feud between religious and military powers in the Middle East, their tactics are much closer to each other than you would think.

He chuckled and said, "Don't worry, we know how to handle the Salafis."

You see, the Muslim Brotherhood were well organized and they recognized that if they got the Salafis on their side, the sheer volume of their supporters would allow them to win the elections.

Al-Shater marveled at how he manipulated Salafis in the parliament. "They are very easy to deal with," he said. "They try to put up a lot of obstacles about how the laws are not 'Islamic enough.' For example, we needed to approve a loan from abroad and they wouldn't approve it because they think interest rates are haram, so we reapplied the law and called the rates 'Islamic deeds' and we were able to get it approved."

My god, I was sitting with a con artist! This is how they intended to control the country. Religion when needed, business when appropriate, and deception all the time.

"Are you actually bragging about duping your Salafi colleagues in the parliament?"

The others in the room grew restless.

"I am trying to tell you that they are not as dangerous as you think. Now, let me continue with our vision of the Renaissance Project—"

"You didn't answer my question about using religion," I interrupted. "What you have told me is not convincing, and I find it hard to trust you guys if you continue using the same tired technique."

"We are not here to discuss Sharia, we are here to discuss the project and how we adopted it from other successful countries," he responded sharply.

"Well, since we are talking about successful countries," I said, "none of those countries have Sharia Law and they are doing fine."

"You can't draw similarities between Egypt and other countries. Every country is different," he answered.

"Well, you just did. By giving examples of other countries, you bring their whole experience to the table, you can't just pick and choose," I said.

And then—*bam!*—he slammed his hand on the table. "Listen," he said impatiently, "what is the percentage of the Islamic block in the parliament?"

"What does this have to do with anything?" I asked.

"Answer me, what is the percentage?"

"Well, seventy-five percent," I replied.

"The people have chosen," he said decisively. "We have the majority. The people want religion."

"So what are we doing here then?" I asked. "It is obvious that you don't need the twenty-five percent minority. Good luck with your majority. History is full of others like you who got arrogant because of percentage points and statistics and masses cheering for them in the streets. Many of them wish they would have listened to much calmer voices who didn't cheer their every move. But why would you be any different?"

We left the building as the confused eyes of his subordinates followed us.

Right in front of the Brotherhood headquarters I lost my cool.

I barked at Tarek, "This is the guy your father wanted me to meet? He is a fucking asshole. You think Mubarak was a dictator? This guy is worse, much worse, he is going to fuck us all once they get to power."

Tarek wanted to remove me from there since we were still outside their building and he was scared someone would hear us.

At that point I lost all hope that anything good could come out of the Brotherhood. Even Tarek, despite his family roots, was disappointed after that meeting.

Those guys were on a next-level power trip and were happy with their majority in the parliament.

As presidential elections approached, there was a final count of thirteen candidates. The only "Islamic" candidate was Mohamed Morsi, the one who had been used as a puppet by al-Shater. There were others with different backgrounds and even some with previously Islamic backgrounds, but Morsi was the true Islamic candidate.

You would think that Morsi would have won from the first round, wouldn't you? Well, he managed to get only 25 percent. This was a huge blow for the Islamists. After killing it in every election and referendum, they saw that their popularity was diminishing.

All the same, Morsi still managed to be the top candidate, but only by three points. There was going to be a final run-off vote between the top two candidates. He was closely trailed by the previous prime minister under Mubarak, Ahmed Shafik (I know too many alien Arabic names). They would have a head-to-head final showdown.

The shift of the Muslim Brotherhood's behavior was truly interesting. After being so arrogant and pompous they went back to "apologize" to the "comrades of the square," and went around begging for support. They called me and many others and asked us to support Morsi to beat the representative of the old regime. Many of the liberal camp, you know, the 20 to 25 percent who were previously unneeded, took the bait—not because they liked Morsi or believed the Muslim Brotherhood, but because many considered that the first freely elected president after the revolution should not be the prime minister who symbolically represented the old regime.

Morsi won by 51 percent. He couldn't have won without the "insignificant minority" they always belittled.

Sure enough, after he and the Brotherhood won, they did what they do best: screwed everyone over. Let the games begin!

MORSI WAS NOW THE REALITY THAT WE HAD TO DEAL WITH. STILL in a daze from my visit to *The Daily Show*, I realized I had to get my shit together as quickly as possible.

We finally managed to sign the contract with CBC for the new season. Most of the media experts continued to laugh at us and count the days for us to flop. I decided to ignore the critics and march forward. The only thing that mattered was to make sure no one interfered with our content.

It was time to think big: bigger team, bigger production, and bigger theater. We found a deserted theater in the middle of Cairo only a quarter of a mile from Tahrir Square. A beautiful prime location where we could smell the tear gas every time there were further clashes in the square. Everything needed to be renovated, as the building had lain vacant for fifteen years. This was a great way to start our project—by telling our investors that we had chosen a location that was in danger of vandalism and destruction from day one.

People continued to make fun of us because we were putting all this effort into a weekly show, but I didn't care. I was too busy trying to build a completely new team. In Egypt we don't have regular writers for news shows. Mostly what we have are part-time journalists who write summaries of the day's events for the anchors to comment on. That's Egyptian television. It was like trying to build a car in a country with no infrastructure for a decent industry.

I picked writers from Facebook and Twitter. We hired young researchers, again none who had worked in media before. With so many amateurs on board, we had the same chance of succeeding as a nine-year-old at a Texas Hold'em tournament in Vegas.

The technical front was a disaster. We had a problem with live editing and how to do it in the theater. The production team tried three different companies to make this work, but they all failed. We didn't have a single company in the region who specialized in that kind of technology, so we had to train people who'd been in the industry for years on how to do the live edits.

The time was approaching for our debut on television and everyone was anticipating it—either waiting for us to break out big or fail miserably.

On the political front, again many accused me of selling out. A year earlier I had been the dog that belonged to the Christian billionaire. Now I was the dog of a shady owner of a shady corporation who was hiring faces from old media. The only constant was the dog part. You can never win.

Part of me was motivated by the fact that I wanted to impress Jon Stewart. The way he celebrated me and my team and my pledge to make a live-audience political satire show for the first time in the Arab world was my driving force. I dreamed that one day he would visit me in my theater and would be proud. Everyone laughed at me when I told them that, the same way they had laughed at me when I said I would take an abandoned theater and create a live show. I had a lot to prove, even to myself.

A MOVIE THAT REALLY "BOMBED"

It was September 2012 when a group of people discovered they were fans of the Prophet Muhammad and decided to show their admiration by depicting his life in a short movie. Only problem was, they depicted him in the most unflattering way, as a crazy rapist pedophile who preached violence. Of course, many Muslims reacted predictably: they burned stuff.

A group of Christian Egyptian Americans who had been living in the States for decades basically duped a group of American actors into making this biopic. It was a D-grade movie, not even good enough for a DVD release. So they did the second-best thing and released it on YouTube instead. That way the whole world could appreciate its horrible quality . . . Multiple death threats later, the American actors claimed that they were wrongly briefed about the movie and participated in something different from what they were promised.

If there was a sort of World Cup of lost opportunities, Muslims should have taken first, second, and last place because instead of using this as a way to reach out and change stereotypes, they went ballistic. Isn't it a wonder that when people accuse Islam and its Prophet of being violent and extreme, the first reaction out of Muslims is violence and extremism? It's like pointing a gun to someone's head and shouting, "How dare you say I am not peaceful!"

Egypt had its own noob cipher of a Fox News talking head in Khaled Abdullah, who dedicated hours to talking about this piece-of-shit movie. He would show parts of it while mourning the idea that Muslims had submitted to the evil powers of America.

The movie on YouTube hardly had over a thousand views initially, but in two days, thanks to Khaled "Sean Hannity" Abdullah, the views jumped to 3 million. Anger erupted all over the Islamic world. Many American buildings were attacked, including those in Libya. This was the prequel of the Benghazi attack. You've heard it directly from a Middle Easterner now, so Republicans can find someone else other than Hillary Clinton to blame.

America was demonized just because a few people carrying its passport made the movie. It kind of sucks when you are blamed for the action of the stupid few, right? Now you know how I feel when a terrorist attack occurs and the shooter is a Muslim. Further demonstrations and even attacks on American embassies occurred all over the region. Our brothers in Sudan were very creative: it seems they got confused and attacked the German embassy and burned its flag. I'm sure the pre-planning session went something like this: "Is that the American embassy?" "Yeah, the flag is colorful enough, it looks Western." "Cool, burn it down."

In Egypt, riots erupted in downtown Cairo, outside the American embassy. The embassy was attacked and even had its walls breached by people carrying al-Qaeda flags. The spokesman of the Salafi Al Nour party didn't denounce the attack and even justified the anger while he demonized America as an evil imperial power. Three years later he was finishing his MPA at Harvard. He wanted to get a degree from the same school as *Legally Blonde*'s Elle Woods.

I was only a few weeks away from starting my live show, and then, I got an email. It was from the producers of *The Daily Show*.

They wanted me to do a piece via Skype as a Middle Eastern correspondent commenting on what was happening.

What???

Jon wanted *me* to be on his show again—not as a guest, but as a *correspondent*. I couldn't believe it. Only a few weeks earlier I was a total unknown to the American audience and now I was being asked to be part of my dream show?

This was too good to be true . . .

Well, that's exactly what it was!

The script was hilarious. It was about me giving an explanation of what was happening with all these Muslims, reminding Jon that Islam was a younger religion than Christianity and Judaism and it was just going through puberty. Christianity and Judaism have already gone through their rebellious phases. Judaism with its ancient weird rules and destructive wars and Christianity with the Inquisition and the Crusades. Now it was Islam's turn to become a man. There were a lot of references to adolescent problems ranging from acne to bad sex. The satire was great, and I was incredibly excited to do it. I agreed on a time to be on-air with them via Skype.

I sent the script to my publicists, who fired back at me, "Are you out of your mind? Do you think you can make all of those insinuations in the middle of this terrifying riot? You think people will leave you alone?"

They were right. There was a lot of anger. And as you know, angry people, especially religious ones, don't have much of a sense of humor. But I was blinded by the amazing opportunity to be on Jon's show.

It was only two hours to airtime, and after too much contemplation I sent them a long email apologizing for not being able to make it. The stakes were too high and this could be a PR disaster. I was thinking Jon would hate me forever and never talk to me again.

Then half an hour later, my phone rang. It was Jon. First thing he said was "Don't do it, you should be safe." I continued to apologize, but he was very understanding. This was one of many times that I saw his humanity; he wasn't just some performer. Two years later he would again advise me to stop my own show for my safety. Apparently comedy does have some boundaries.

They played the piece anyway, with John Oliver taking "my" spot. Damn you, Oliver!

Till this day it is a mystery as to why those bearded men openly demonstrated with al-Qaeda flags in the streets and got too close for comfort to the American embassy. The Salafi faces who incited the hate were all on the side of the army when they removed the Muslim Brotherhood a couple of years later. The police and military forces who would usually crack down on anyone who would get within two blocks of the embassy virtually disappeared from the streets. Something was off and in the moment I couldn't put my finger on it.

It's a wonder how blinded we were toward everything as it was happening. It seemed that everything was falling apart: the country, the live-show preparations, and even my marriage.

IT TAKES EIGHTY-
TWO TO TANGO

At this point it is fair to say that my wife got cheated in this marriage.

We met in 2010 while I was still a heart surgeon. At that time I had hobbies other than making fun of TV pundits and politicians. I was a dancer. I loved to dance all my life, and I even used to teach Argentinian tango and salsa. In a conservative country like Egypt, a guy who takes up dancing as his pastime and even as a source of income is frowned upon—especially within an even more conservative community like doctors. Some of my senior colleagues and medical school professors used that against me. It didn't matter how good or bad I was as a doctor, the dancing was brought up at every turn. I didn't care, though. I didn't censor myself to please them and I didn't give up what I liked to earn their approval. Maybe I had a rebellious streak all along. A rebel with a Latin beat!

I always felt that if I married, I would marry a woman who appreciated what I did and even be part of it. Then came my wife, Hala, to perfectly complement me. We both loved tango and had a passion for the arts. It didn't take long to seal the deal and get married at the end of 2010.

We hosted tango nights in our house, went to classes together, and even spent our honeymoon at a tango festival. A few weeks after that, the whole revolution thing happened. I found myself time-sucked into the YouTube show, then the TV show, and then the preparation for the live show with all of the political turmoil that came with it. Things got horrendously dark and busy.

"I married a tango-dancing doctor, not an absentee TV celebrity," she used to tell me at the dinner table.

With my newfound fame, and since the show started airing, I was never there for her. I spent all my time in the theater, supervising the renovation and getting ready for the big debut.

Our team rapidly expanded. We now had a staff of eighty-two people. Yup, I counted them: producers, writers, researchers, technicians, and everyone in between. I was responsible for the biggest production in Egyptian television history, all while the Islamists rose to power and my marriage suffered.

Till this day I don't know why my wife stayed. She once told me that if I were another celebrity she would have just walked out. But she believed in what I was doing. She too was part of a younger generation that was sick and tired of decades of taboos and the suppression of free thought. "This is not just another show, it is a statement and people need it," my wife told me. I guess some men are luckier than others!

MY BIG DAY
(OR HOW GREAT SHOWS COME WITH GREATER INSULTS)

For weeks, while rebuilding a theater out of scratch, tech rehearsals continued for hours each day. We were struggling with everything, from playing videos in real time to queuing photos and graphics over my shoulder. Nothing was working. I was losing my head every time something went wrong. Eventually we started incorporating and practicing the script. Because of the incessant production interruptions we didn't even know if we had a comedic show anymore.

Funny or not, the big day was here. When I had attended Jon's show, they had a comedian who would warm the audience up beforehand. He would tell the audience to cheer and laugh and clap so the people at home would feel energized. But you couldn't do that here. If you tell Egyptians to laugh or clap they do the opposite . . . because we are just too cool for that! I had to hope that we had created an entertaining show.

I stood backstage waiting for my cue to enter the stage. I didn't want to mess up or do retakes. Khalifa, the director, spoke in my earpiece to give me the countdown.

Then . . . *showtime!*

The lights, the applause, the excitement: What the hell was I doing all that time taping boring pre-recorded shows?

I took my seat. Here I was a doctor, a surgeon, whose only theater before now was an operating theater where I used to cut people open. Nothing in my life had prepared me for this. I never received any formal comedic training, or any training in improv or acting—nothing. In my earpiece I could hear Khalifa and Hend giving final orders. Tarek was in the front row. All of those people who, months earlier, doubted I'd ever make it past the first week of the first season of a small show with a limited budget were watching, judging.

I MADE MY FIRST QUIP ABOUT TRYING TO JUSTIFY HOW I ENDED up on this channel, which I admitted was for one reason and one reason alone: money. I went on to tear down every single person working for the network, including the owner. The theater erupted in laughter. They couldn't believe I was going there, and I couldn't believe that my jokes were landing. I continued on a more treacherous path, deciding to go after the almighty Muslim Brotherhood. I dissected their rhetoric and destroyed their beloved Renaissance Project, and I showed people how they were using religion to manipulate the masses. What I was hearing in that theater was not laughter; it was catharsis.

One joke after the other, one video after another, I was killing it out there. That first episode lasted more than ninety minutes, which I had never thought I could pull off. It was amazing.

When the show ended I went offstage where everyone jumped on me and hugged me: Amr, Khalifa, Hend, Tarek, every single one of the crew who attended the boring rehearsals and doubted this would ever take off. I was drenched in sweat and out of breath as if I'd run a race. *What the hell just happened?*

The history of Egyptian television was changed forever. In the next few months everyone in the media wanted to do a "Bassem

Youssef–type show." Live-audience shows started emerging out of nowhere. But our audience came of their own free will; they were never paid and their reactions were unrehearsed. Our weekly show became a regional phenomenon.

As expected, the Muslim Brotherhood lashed out against me. They didn't care about the daily demonstrations against them, or journalists and TV hosts criticizing them. They were worried about me more than anything. Authoritarian regimes, whether military or religious, are not worried about vicious criticism. They are worried that the masses lose respect for them. You can't really respect or fear something you are laughing at.

But the greatest attack came from within the channel itself. The oldest, most veteran TV anchor was upset because I had made fun of him. He represented a form of neoliberal authoritarianism, an older generation that wasn't used to being criticized. He went on his show and attacked me, but made the fatal mistake of trying to be funny. After belittling me, calling me all kinds of derogatory names, he threatened that he would shut down my show. Well, two could play this game, and I had the upper comedic hand. So I decided to go after him in my next episode. It was nothing personal, but if I didn't respond it meant that anyone could bash me into silence and I didn't want to set that precedent. This was me getting my TV cred! This was me going after that old mentality that built its glory on faux respect. The channel executives didn't want to piss off their oldest and most famous TV host. He was a media dinosaur but his name was still a big deal, so they asked me to let it go. I said I just couldn't do that.

My next episode was all about how Morsi was turning into a dictator. I told the network that I found it weird that they were more worried about the feelings of their anchor than they were about me going after the president. They suggested that we visit the anchor in his house and ask for his permission to be mentioned in the next episode. I was furious. I told them I would do no such thing. Tarek urged me to play along. "We have only broadcast a pilot, we can't afford to stop the show now," he said. "I beg you, be nice and be polite and I promise you that you will get to do what you want."

The deal was that everyone would be there and that the owner of the channel would be the one who broke the news about me joking back. The owner promised me that whatever the outcome I could broadcast the episode as I wanted, but still asked me to do this "courtesy visit" to the anchor first.

We went to his stupid house. He represented everything that I hated about our culture: the patriarchical mentality, the entitlement, the arrogance that came from the fact that he had wasted more years on this planet than the rest of us. He gave me a "lesson" on respecting my elders and how it was not acceptable to make fun of them. Just to give you an idea, this man was supposed to be the "Godfather" of the new Arab media. He was the one who bragged about how he was more knowledgeable about Western media than anyone else. He owned the first private radio station and entertainment website in Egypt. He was also a close friend of Mubarak, which partly explains why he was given the privilege to spew all of his "knowledge."

I reminded him that in the "Western media" there is no person above satire and sarcasm. He didn't accept any of this and continued to give me a lesson about respect and morality (three years later, this guy would escape from Egypt after allegedly amassing millions of dollars through bribes and shady deals with the media outlets he worked for—respect and morality, my ass!).

I sat there waiting for the owner of the channel to speak about the next episode. Of course, he pussied out. No one else spoke. So now it was up to me to tell him what I intended to do in that episode. The brontosaurus lost his shit! He told me that if I ever mentioned his name, let alone made fun of him, he would personally see to it that my career was ruined. He added, in English, "Mark my words, I will personally fuck you!" *Ooo kinky!*

We left the house. And right there in the street I told the owner in a calm voice that I would do this episode the way I wanted, and that if he didn't like it he could terminate my contract. Tarek was not amused.

The next day I went to the office and finalized a special script about my dear stegosaurus friend, which became the second segment of the episode. The first was dedicated to my other good buddies, the Muslim Brotherhood.

They were using the Salafis to reshape the constitution to make it more Islamic. Morsi had prevented the Supreme Court from putting obstacles in the way of the new constitution. What was worse was how the Muslim Brotherhood had ordered its people to surround the Supreme Court building. They camped around it for weeks and prevented the judges from going in. This was a full-militia exploit. Since the police wouldn't help him, he had his faithful soldiers do the dirty work.

The pilot of our show was a revolution that rippled throughout the television world. But the second episode was a revolutionary wave that railed against everything authoritarian. I crushed that veteran anchor, I personally went after Morsi, and I spared no sarcasm when skewering the Muslim Brotherhood and their militias.

I did that at the risk of the channel terminating my contract and also at the risk of going to jail. An article of Egyptian law that still existed from the Mubarak days stated you could go to jail for "insulting the president." This is how Egyptian laws are: subjective, extremely ambiguous, and innovative in the ways in which they can lock you up and lose the key.

The channel didn't air the episode, to avoid upsetting their anchor. Their explanation for the cancellation was because of "live coverage of street clashes." People didn't buy it. We went ahead and put it on YouTube as a little virtual *fuck you*. The views of this episode were in the millions. It was a lesson for the channel that censorship wouldn't work with me. Under pressure from the audience, the channel backpedaled. They saw the viewership on YouTube going through the roof and everyone talking about this new show, and couldn't afford not to air us.

That day, the establishment bowed its head to the will of the people. No more "moral police" dictating what people should watch anymore.

The show was now too powerful to be stopped. People gathered to watch it in cafés, like Super Bowl games. They didn't watch us simply because we were funny, though. They watched us because they saw hope in the show—hope to challenge long-standing taboos and authority, whether that authority came in the form of a beard, or a tank, or a codger demanding, "Respect your elders."

RISKY BUSINESS

CONDOMS, ALCOHOL, AND ROCK AND ROLL

DECEMBER 2012

Legend has it that the only populist power in the country were the Islamists and that the "others" were merely a weak minority. We were the "others." We were the ones the Muslim Brotherhood needed to win the election by a mere 1 percent. We were used as a tool for them to get the presidency, and when they won they broke every promise they made us.

Islamists were fighting for a divine cause but we liberals were viewed as wusses who had nothing left in us to fight for our cause . . . maybe because other than not wanting to be ruled by religious dogma or a military dictatorship and seeking equality for all and other hippie principles, we hadn't really settled on a clearly defined cause. How can you compare trivial causes like human rights and freedom with a divine cause like fighting for Allah (whatever the fight was) or fighting for the country (even if the ones claiming to fight were in bed with all your enemies)?

The "true" liberal powers saw that they were duped and started calling for nationwide protests. (I use *true* because later we will discover that many so-called liberals turned out to be fascists. They just preferred the whip of the military to the sword of the Islamists.)

Anyways, hundreds of thousands of disgruntled anti-Islamist protestors organized in front of the presidential palace. They had had it with the manipulation of the constitution and how Islamists were breaking one promise after another. Many of the demonstrators left at the end of the day and went home, but a few hundred stayed behind for a sit-in. When the numbers began to dwindle, the Muslim Brotherhood sent their militias to attack them.

Many were killed that night, but the violence wasn't between citizens and police. It was between protestors and Muslim Brotherhood militias. Even when the Brotherhood were in power, they couldn't get the militia mentality out of their mind. This happened a few hours before taping our episode.

Egypt was living through one tragedy after another. People were killed every day because of something. This became our own Columbine reality on a weekly basis. There was always this challenge of trying to make people laugh amid such terrible circumstances. But what could we do? If we closed up shop every time Egypt lived through another tragedy or unrighteous killing, we might as well not have a show at all. Nonetheless, my team implored me to cancel the show. They were worried about how we would be perceived. I was already stressed out because I still wasn't used to the timing of a live program and found myself shouting in the control room, "I can't just go and cancel the show every other episode! This is the country we are living in. Death has become a mere statistic. You will always find trolls who will say to you, how dare you laugh at whatever tragedy is going on in the country. Well, guess what, the tragedies are about to get worse and the trolls will watch us in secret anyways. There are people out there who need this. I am doing the show."

The footage from the night of the attack was horrific. Many of the demonstrators were tortured by the Muslim Brotherhood militia, and the scenes were graphic and bloody. The anti-Islamic talk shows opted for the sensational angle. They got the most graphic scenes and ran them on repeat. When my researchers were looking for material, they thought they were doing a good job by getting even more graphic and horrific material to show how truly bad the Muslim Brotherhood were. I stopped all of that. "This is a comedy show," I told them. "This is not another talk show where we aim to be sensational. We need to deal with the worst tragedies and find a way to deliver our message in a way that doesn't repulse people."

They looked at me in bewilderment. *How are we going to find a funny angle in this?*

But we searched again. And this time we were not looking at the news. We were looking for what was behind the news. I directed them to look into the mentality that made these people do what they did. With the police and the army, it was always easier to find their motives. You are armed to the hilt and you receive an order from above to assault, to beat, and to kill. The excuse will always be national security, or the sovereignty of the nation, or any other nationalistic bullshit. But what makes people, normal people, who go with us to the same universities and schools, and even share the same workplaces, view us, the non-Islamists, as targets to be tortured and killed?

We followed the Brotherhood's and the Salafis' shows and their media and aimed to show our viewers what they thought about us. This was not an easy task. Their programs went on for hours. No one actually watched them except their followers. Yet we had to watch the endless hours of bullshit to show the country what kind of sick minds these people had. My team had to endure the same agony Jon Stewart's team had to go through while watching Fox News. Now that's truly torture.

The same sheikhs who would insert and recite Quran verses every couple of sentences in their news reports as a sign of piety were now reporting finding condoms, bottles of Russian vodka, and vaginal douches in the tents of the protestors. "The boys told me they found some of the most expensive liquor called ID 10%," a sheikh said. "Condoms were found in the tents. That's the kind of people we are dealing with."

Hey! Look on the bright side, sheikh: Doesn't that at least mean they are practicing safe sex? Better than having angry protestors running around with herpes!

It's interesting how these "men of God" get worked up about alcohol and sex while they promise their followers unlimited access to rivers of wine and sex with seventy-plus virgins in heaven. It seems you can have fun in the next life but never in this one.

One video after the other with "live coverage" from the battleground showed the Islamists ransacking the tents of the defeated protestors and then holding condoms and empty bottles of alcohol to the camera. It would really take a moron to go out to protest the president while bringing this stuff with them. And it would take an even bigger moron to believe the Islamist media's lies.

I was happy with what we did with the episodes that followed this disaster. We didn't show a single graphic scene. We didn't play the victim card. We didn't show the horribly violent clashes. We were true to the message of sarcasm and comedy, and yet we did what no other "serious" show or news outlet dared to do: we exposed those people for who they were. We showed the sick mentality that was driving these insane actions. It was easy to make people hate them, but more important, we showed how absolutely trivial they were.

After those attacks, and with the continuous exposure of their hateful media, the reign of the Islamists seemed to weaken, at least in many major cities, whereas previously any Islamist figure with an al-Qaeda-style beard was considered untouchable. But now those "men of God" were losing their credibility and people were waking up. Now a common name was given to them—"religion dealers." It was a degrading term used to describe all those with religious authority who profit from religion. Think of your typical crooked televangelists, à la Jimmy Swaggart, and you get the picture.

I went after them in every episode and they didn't like it. They in turn dedicated most of their airtime to attacking me. They used whatever religious fatwas they could to deem my show as haram. (Hey! Look at you understanding two Arabic words in one sentence now. Way to go!)

In one episode I showed another aspect of how these Islamist minds worked. Part of being a good Muslim was to be decent and respectful and not insult other people, even if they smeared you or called you names. That whole "do unto others" mentality. Yet, it was a constant spectacle to hear and watch the worse kind of smear campaigns and the lowest kind of behavior of these Islamists toward Christians and even other Muslims who didn't follow their dogma.

The way I ended the episode helped many people see things differently.

I said, "You keep calling us infidels, unworthy of being good Muslims. You know what? We are fine with that. We are through trying to make you happy because there is actually no point in doing so. We will not be put through your guilt trips anymore. You see, it's a very simple equation: if we are not Muslims in your eyes, well, you are not sheikhs, scholars, or men of religion in ours. You are preaching a religion that we don't know and don't want to be part of. Keep that religion to yourself and we will keep ours."

Those couple of minutes of the show were replayed over and over again on television and online. They offered emancipation for many young people looking for a way out of this eternal religious struggle. As simple as it might seem, this was new for our region to stand up to the tyranny of the religious mafia. Despite being in power, they *had* no power over us anymore. Whatever respect they had was diminishing in the hearts and minds of the people. And the people "in charge" didn't try to make it better. They just kept on doing what they did best: becoming more arrogant, alienating everyone, and in the process heading full speed to their own demise.

THE CURIOUS CASE OF ABU ISMAIL

Think of a zealous religious conservative like Mike Huckabee with his extreme fundamentalist quotes and his adorable smile. Then add some Michelle Bachman's non-fact "facts." Then mix that with the bigotry of Donald Trump and the self-serving beliefs of Ted Cruz. Then go ahead and wrap everything up in the crazy that is Sarah Palin. Add a dash of twisted religious interpretation and a scary Islamic beard and now you have Abu Ismail.

Hazem Salah Abu Ismail was an Islamist leader. He didn't officially belong to any political party or group, but instead managed to create a cult of his own.

He had one of those Santa Claus/ISIS beards growing out of, I kid you not, an adorable baby face. He was in his sixties, but without the beard he looked exactly like Paul McCartney in the 1960s. He was a lawyer, but on the side he had a more lucrative job. He was a television sheikh with his own spot in one of the mosques downtown.

He was a different kind of sheikh. He didn't just speak about good and bad deeds, heaven and hell, or any of those regular topics about religious rituals and chores. He thought of himself as a different brand. He preached what we can call "bullshit applied religion." He specialized in speaking about matters that are important to a bigoted Muslim, such as how the Western world is a degenerate filthy place that is trying to destroy Islam in every possible way.

He was known for his ability to uncover the Western conspiracies against Islam. One of his famous television lessons showed him explaining that the soda company Pepsi had led a conspiracy. Yes, Pepsi. The one related to child obesity, sugar addiction, and Beyoncé. He said that Pepsi was an acronym for *Pay Every Penny to Save Israel*.

I will give you a moment to digest all of this . . . Okay, we're back.

He was out there spreading a utopian image of the Islamic empire; we ruled the world because we were better Muslims. For the likes of Abu Ismail, a vibrant era is only measured by the extent of its geography. They don't tell you about the atrocities committed by the many caliphs and war leaders (the same way Christians choose to omit what the Roman and Spanish empires did in the name of Christianity).

When you try to reason with Abu Ismail and his contemporaries, the answer will simply be: *God said it, not me.* You have a problem, take it up with God. And since you don't really have a direct line to God, the sheikh will be the only one with the valid interpretation of God's words.

The rise of Abu Ismail was phenomenal. He organized rallies all over the country. The turnout of his supporters was absolutely crazy. What was special about him is that he didn't try to sugarcoat his words. He didn't play the political game the Muslim Brotherhood played when asked about issues like equality, women's rights, minorities, and personal freedom. People liked him because he was "not politically correct, he spoke his mind and told it like it is." Again—sound familiar?

This was apparent in how he discussed a topic like the hijab. Many Islamic scholars refuse to admit that the Islamic faith forces women to wear it. Alternatively, they still guilt them into wearing it. Abu Ismail laid it out plain and simple: "In the army you can't just wear anything you want. You need to wear the uniform that your leaders dictate to you. So if God, the leader of all leaders, tells you to wear the hijab, you do it. Or else you are not a part of his ranks and in turn you are not a Muslim. You are a defector. This is an act of mutiny." We all know what happens to defectors, right? (Make slashing sound with finger as you drag it across your throat.)

The beautiful thing about these people is that they sound as if they are giving you a choice. "You either do it or you are not considered a Muslim." This is the definition of entrapment.

I desperately tried to host Abu Ismail on my show. I saw one anchor after another fail to confront his bullshit. He could talk ad nauseam and just make things up because the anchors didn't know any better. Mainly because they didn't really have a solid background in Islamic history. Now, I was raised in a conservative family, and my father's job as a judge required him to be knowledgeable about Islamic and civil society. I enjoyed reading a lot about history and how Islam has evolved, thanks in part to my father's huge library. I could see right through this guy.

I finally got through to one of his close followers or apprentices. He told me that the "sheikh" was too busy but I could come meet him and then we'd take it from there.

I went to his house and waited outside in my car. His apprentice told me that he needed to get going to a rally in a town about a two-hour drive away. "He could go with you in the car and you can discuss his appearance with you."

So for the next two hours I doubled as a chauffeur and as a fixer trying to get him on the show. He sat next to me with two of his closest followers in the backseat.

The guy was very sweet. He talked in a low voice in a respectful way. His ideology was a disaster, though. It was like having a polite conversation with a serial killer.

I didn't want to confront him on his issues because I didn't want to alienate him from coming onto the show. But every time I questioned some of his ISIS-like thoughts, he'd say, "I didn't make this up, they are only God's words." I tried to maintain the "stupid anchor" character so he would think I was an easy target and come on the show.

But then we got on the topic of the rights of religious minorities. "You don't accept that other people from different faiths have the right to promote their beliefs in public, do you?" I asked him.

"It is an Islamic country. Only Islam should be promoted openly. Yet we should love and care for our Christian brothers," he said.

"Then why do many Islamists whine when one Western country bans the burqa or one European city doesn't issue a permit to build a mosque? Why do you welcome and take advantage of the fact that any Muslim can stand in the middle of any major city in America or Europe promoting Islam but you don't accept the same for others here?"

That was a stupid mistake. I could see his followers in the back-seat frown as I asked. He never lost his smile. He said some bullshit excuses like every country is different and cultures are not alike, and then changed the subject.

I knew right then that I had lost my chance. Two hours for nothing.

We arrived at the rally, where at least ten thousand people had come to receive him. He was greeted like a rock star as he came onto the stage.

Some of them recognized me. They liked the show and followed me closely. They thought I was funny but hoped that I would take it a little easier on Islam. To them, the likes of Abu Ismail represented *real* Islam. I watched the rally from a distance with thousands of men cheering on his racist ideas as he laid them out with the biggest of smiles.

Over the next few months this guy's popularity skyrocketed. Thousands of followers were showing up at his rallies, and I was shocked to find that well-educated people were embracing his message. To be fair, he was vocal against the military. Young people loved that. They were growing tired of the revolution being in standstill mode, so they chose a guy who revolted against military dictatorship, and hoped to replace it with an Islamic military dictatorship. For some reason many ignored the second part of the equation.

Hazem Abu Ismail eventually ran for president. It was scary to find someone with his mentality and popularity having a shot at the presidency. There was only one, technical problem. In Egypt, to run for president, you and your immediate family could not carry another nationality.

He was disqualified when it was found that his mother and sister were living in the United States and held American passports, and as we all know by now, America is a horrible-no-good-very-bad country.

PROSTITUTING
AN ANCIENT
CIVILIZATION

One of the advantages (and disadvantages) of democracy is that stupid people have the same freedom to speak up. After the revolution the Islamists expressed what was really on their minds, and it was like giving them the rope with which to hang themselves. Thoughts that were discussed for decades only in their closed circles were surfacing freely on the airwaves.

Out of nowhere the Islamists started to attack the pharaohs. Yes, you got that right. They were attacking people who had been dead for thousands of years. A Salafi went on television calling for the Sphinx to be destroyed and for the pyramids to be demolished. He claimed that these were idols and should be destroyed like the Buddha statues in Afghanistan. While he could be viewed as a crazy man who had no weight and no real merit in the Islamist community, when we at the show dug deep, we found very interesting opinions about the issue from their well-known and more popular leaders. The principles and the dogma were one and the same as those of the crazy extremists in Afghanistan or ISIS. The only difference was that the Islamist leaders were diplomatic when they spoke about our ancient civilization. No matter how smart you think you are, your bat-shit crazy opinions could surface and come back to haunt you.

The stupidity went beyond that Salafi guy with plans to destroy the pyramids. It ran deep into Islamist history. In the past, people used God and Islam as excuses to destroy whatever human heritage there was, under the pretense of the monuments or objects being pagan. In all honesty, the Muslim Brotherhood leaders didn't share the same stupid opinions, at least not openly. But when you are running on an "Islam is the solution" slogan and your biggest ally in the elections and in writing the constitution are Salafis, you risk the generalization. It especially doesn't help when you are an Islamic authority and you generalize against your opponents, calling them degenerate, sex-hungry liberals. Well, it goes both ways. So when one of your allies speaks in favor of pedophile marriages and female genital mutilation, and allows for the harassment of women because she "brought it on herself by not covering up," yet you still join forces with this ally and appear on their TV shows, well, I really don't feel sorry for you. You earned the same stupid reputation.

Anyway, back to the pharaohs. My show's researchers unearthed more videos and stumbled upon a Salafi party leader who had run for parliament in the recent elections saying that the pharaohs' civilization was rotten. He went on to espouse that since Islam had entered Egypt, we didn't need to study or care about this ancient "rotten" civilization that worshiped stones and idols. I commented that it is true, if it wasn't for Islam entering Egypt we would all be stuck in Cairo's horrible traffic on a daily basis trying to get to the pyramids to show our respect and give our offering to our pharaoh gods. Thank goodness we could call to prayer from the comfort of our own homes.

Islamists were up in arms against me, saying that I had taken the Salafi leader's words out of context. So I got more videos of him saying that we should ban receiving money from tourism at our ancient Egyptian monuments because it was haram, and if we really needed to keep those statues we could just put wax masks over them to hide their features. That was a brilliant idea, of course! I suggested why not put masks in the form of his lovely, bearded, peaceful face? Surely it wouldn't melt under the hot Egyptian sun.

We then got more videos of one of the most credible and respected Salafi leaders suggesting that early Muslims, when they originally took on Egypt, should have destroyed the pharaonic temples and statues.

There was one problem, though; the pyramids and the temples were buried under the sand and it was because of the French invasion of Egypt at the end of the eighteenth century that these monuments were unearthed. So basically the early Muslims didn't see them and if they did, the "Muslim thing" would be to destroy them. Thank god for sand!

You might think that only the backward Salafi sheikhs were in on this ridiculousness. But it was more of a general way of thinking. As a matter of fact, a "serious" Islamist researcher, with a suit and tie instead of your typical Taliban-like outfit, came out and claimed that the pyramids were built through money paid in return for sexual favors! He said that the daughters of the three kings who built the famous three pyramids of Giza slept with men for money that was later used to finance the building of the pyramids. Given that there are more than two million stones in the Great Pyramid alone, well, that's a lot of sex. Imagine if the pharaohs continued to rule, we would have built a totally new infrastructure through our harem of royal hos.

When we hear now that ISIS is demolishing a temple or demolishing thousands of heritage sites, it doesn't come out of nothing. They all come from the same pitiful, extreme source. In Egypt, the Islamists, despite choosing their words carefully, still managed to show their real face.

This is actually why I have a bit more respect for the Salafis than the Muslim Brotherhood. At least they are straightforward with their stupidity and bigotry. They are our Muslim rednecks. They are the ones waiting for the Rapture and have no problem showing their hate and disdain for others. The Muslim Brotherhood are just power whores sugarcoating their extreme views with fake political correctness, but when you pull back the curtain they behave like any regular Muslim hillbilly.

Their sugarcoating and "tolerance" couldn't hold up forever. Something had to give. They went after their enemies, and I was one of them.

HOW TO INTERROGATE A JOKER

"There is a warrant for your arrest," my lawyer told me on the phone.

Since day one of the live tapings we were bombarded with accusations and legal complaints against the program. We had around forty-two legal complaints against us at the office of the general prosecutor. So far the prosecutor had moved none of them forward. You see, the way it works here, people place their complaints, but it is up to the prosecutor whether or not to move forward into an actual investigation. Some of the accusations were ridiculous—like the complaint accusing me of tarnishing the relationship with a friendly country, Pakistan. Up to that point, I didn't know we had such a sensitive relationship with Pakistan, and I didn't know how friendly Pakistan was with us. The joke that got me in trouble, though? It was not even a joke. It was a hat.

President Morsi in a visit to Pakistan received an honorary doctorate. The university that was honoring him had a peculiar academic outfit. He was dressed in a fancy graduation gown and hood, but the hat was so fucking funny that we made a replica of it. The only difference was, we made it three feet tall and it weighed forty pounds. I made my entrance onto the stage wearing this monstrosity in the episode following his visit to Pakistan. That gigantic hat became the most iconic prop piece in Arab television history. We had to put it in the lobby of the theater for people to take pictures with it. But in the end, that hat, coupled with other jokes, pissed off the wrong people.

The general prosecutor finally took action. The charges?

1. Insulting the president. *Of course.*
2. Insulting Islam. *Sure.*
3. Spreading profanity and destroying the fabric of society. *I don't even know what that is.* Speaking of fabric, we do have fine Egyptian cotton, though.
4. Disturbing the social peace. *Seriously, who comes up with this crap?*

In Egypt, it is enough to go to the prosecutor to say that you have been psychologically affected by anything someone says or does and file a complaint. It sounds comical but in reality, if the government wants this to fly, it will fly. The accusations themselves were maddeningly vague. How do you disturb the peace? How do you destroy the fabric of society? Scissors? But believe it or not, many have been arrested on similar charges. The laws in this patriarchal society can send you to jail for simply not behaving well. Which is extremely subjective.

The one charge that I was worried about was "insulting Islam." This was the single, most disturbing charge that could not be defended against. The people sending you to jail may not even be religious, but the charge was an amazing tool to round up the masses against someone. If you are labeled as someone who disrespects Islam it is like having an opponent with a royal flush in a game of poker. Nothing beats it, there is no trump card. This is a charge that no one would dare defend you against because it would put them in the same box of "Islam enemies."

Soon it was all over the news. My ever-worrying mom called me in hysterics. She was afraid that police officers would take me right to jail.

An emergency meeting was called at the theater. My lawyer and partners all came to discuss what was happening.

It was a Monday. The biggest concern for my lawyer was that the police would come to arrest me in my house at night. My biggest concern was that I wouldn't have time to write the next episode.

We decided that I shouldn't go home that night. I would sleep at the theater and my wife would sleep over at her parents'. We thought that would buy us time to go to the general prosecutor's office the next day willingly, with no officer putting handcuffs on me.

I met with my creative team. "Everything should go as planned," I told them. "We have a show to shoot in forty-eight hours. Unless I don't get back, business continues as usual."

"Can I take your place just this week?" Khaled, one of my writers and fake correspondents, asked loudly.

"No, I should be the one who sits in his chair," Shadi, another fake correspondent and writer, said.

Vultures were already circling!

It was good that everyone was in high spirits and willing to joke. We continued writing and researching late into the night.

I retired to my office alone. I had hardly slept, and by 7 A.M. I was up, ready to willingly turn myself in.

And then it hit me. *I am in show business. Let's make a bit out of this.* I called the prop master and asked him to get the huge hat out. I would go to the general prosecutor's office wearing that hat!

My team, upon hearing of my plan, tried to prevent me from

going. "Dude, are you crazy?" they kept asking me on the phone. The arguments went back and forth. I was sticking to my decision. They could take me to court, they could investigate me, and they could issue a warrant for my arrest—but they'd do it all while I was making them the laughingstock of the country. That's the only weapon I had.

My team arrived at the theater, but none of them walked upstairs to the offices; they all waited for me downstairs. Everyone wanted to come with me to court. I talked to them and told them that, as usual, we were stressed for time. "If they put me in jail, we will have no show," I said, "but what would be worse is if they release me and you guys wasted time while I was gone and we air a bad show. Then they definitely will win."

I made my way to the courthouse. Some of the technical team came along, together with Khalifa (director), Amr (producer), and Abbas (head of communications and the one who would accompany me two years later when I would flee Egypt). The four of us went in one car. Just eighteen months earlier, Khalifa and Amr were in my apartment shooting an Internet episode with a heart surgeon who, outside of his operating room, was a complete no one. Now we were the biggest news in town. We were laughing about that notion as we drove. But as we laughed we knew that it was all for show. Deep down we were terrified.

Many of the technical team followed us in separate cars. The hat was so big they had to rent it its own pickup truck! It was going to be the highlight of my entrance.

We arrived at the courthouse. The streets were packed. Hundreds of people had come out with signs and banners to support me. They were angry at the Islamic government for harassing the "joker."

Dozens of cameras and reporters from everywhere were there

too. The journalists were shouting at me for a comment as I went through the crowd of bodies. This was like the red carpet for a movie premiere, with the slight difference being that I could end up in jail. I, my crew, the reporters, the cameramen, the supporters, the haters, and the security forces were all moving together in an unconventional dance toward the doors of the courthouse.

I tried to keep the biggest smile on my face. With all these cameras, I didn't want a single photo showing me frowning or worried. I didn't want the Islamists to have some disparaging photo of me to put their stupid comments on. I wouldn't give them the satisfaction. I kept waving and smiling, holding the image of a smiling joker in the face of oppression.

As I was pushed, shoved, and herded along in the swarming mass of reporters, I could only think about those TV sheikhs celebrating the day I was "presented" to justice. They wanted to see me broken and defeated. I instructed one of the production assistants to walk behind me while he held the giant "Morsi Hat" above my head. The might of the Islamist government was instantly humiliated by a single silly prop.

I was smiling and laughing and throwing jokes and yet inside I was worried I would not sleep at home that night.

We finally reached the front door of the court. I stood on top of the stairs and put the hat on. Here I was, with a comically tall hat, talking to the crowd through a megaphone. I did a mini–standup routine right there while my fans laughed and my lawyer glared at me angrily. I was making a scene.

An officer told us to follow him to a back entrance into the court. Finally I was inside.

Court employees were coming to take photos and selfies with me as we moved, shouting at me in support. Only one woman came close to me and prayed that God would bring down his rage and vengeance on me. "May you fry in hell!" she shouted. What a good little Muslim she must be!

We arrived at the "interrogation room," which was the office of the chief deputy of the prosecutor. The deputy asked me to sit down. He was a polite, quiet man who weighed three times more than me. In Egypt during interrogations we don't use video cameras or audio recorders. We have the stenographer, who is designated to write down everything as fast as you say it, in the most horrible handwriting. You wonder if it could ever really qualify as evidence.

As we were about to start, several young attorneys came into the room. They were from the general prosecutor's office. They told me they were fans of the show, and started taking photos with me. This was absolutely insane. More police officers came in, asking to take photos with me. The deputy eventually asked them to "get it over with so we can start the interrogation."

We finally started. The deputy asked for the episodes in question so they could play them for me and ask their questions. A middle-aged guy came into the office with a few CDs. He then put one of them into an extremely outdated computer on the deputy's desk. The computer had a Windows 95 operating system and the disks didn't work. I was not surprised. Why would anything work in this place? I tried helping them. I asked them if they had VLC or any other updated version of media player. The whole scene was surreal. I was fucking helping them so they could play video evidence against me! At a certain point I was wondering if they'd downloaded too much porn on that computer and ended up fucking it *completely* (figuratively speaking).

After more than forty-five minutes they gave up trying.

"Okay, so I will just assume that you know your episodes and I will say that we just played the episodes for you," the deputy said. "So we will ask you questions based on the written script as if we played the episodes, okay?"

"Do I have another choice?"

"Not really."

The first question was about the first charge, "insulting Islam." Since we didn't have any videos to play the deputy started to read the transcript from one of my episodes. It was the one in which the Islamist media were celebrating how we now had a pious Islamic president who went to mosques and led the prayers. The Islamists' media circus was all over it, showing different photos of Morsi posing in different prayer stages. In one of our episodes we made a fake infomercial where you could win a place next to the president in a mosque of your choice if you called a certain number. The commercial showed how fast you would go to heaven with all the divine perks if you called the number, let alone the grand prize of meeting the pious president in this amazing spiritual experience.

As the deputy read the script, many in the room started laughing, which continued all throughout the interrogation.

The plan was to play it dumb. "What? Insulting Islam? Me? Never!"

In that same episode we made fun of angry sheikhs who would shout during their sermons at people attending the Friday prayer service. You see, for some reason many sheikhs liked to bring the terror of hell in the afterlife to our mortal doorstep. Imagine a pastor during a Sunday sermon shouting at the top of his lungs, telling you that God would unleash his wrath on you and throw you in a fiery pit, where your skin would melt in front of your eyes. Okay—I get it. That's not that hard to imagine, as we have already demonstrated that radical Christians and radical Muslims are not that different. The only difference where we come from is that we do our shaming sessions on Fridays and you do yours on Sundays. Same scare tactics, different days of the week.

"How is criticizing imams alienating people from Islam considered an insult to Islam?" I asked the deputy.

"Well, many were offended by those jokes," he answered.

"Well, many more are offended on a weekly basis with those who tell us that we are all going to hell," I said in a slightly mocking tone. "Why not bring them here for questioning?"

My lawyer interjected and said, "My client has absolute respect for the Muslim faith and is a Muslim himself. His words were taken out of context and there is no insult to the faith here." He then leaned on my shoulder and whispered, "This is not your theater and these people are not your audience." Then he added firmly, "If you want to get out of here, play along, no need to make big statements. No need to be a hero."

I regurgitated my lawyer's statements in an almost robotic manner. "I had no ill intentions," I said. "I respect the Islamic faith."

The interrogation proceeded to another accusation: "insulting the president." In one of our episodes we showed an exclusive interview with President Morsi, which he gave on the same night as the Academy Awards in Los Angeles. Because of the time difference between Cairo and L.A., the Oscars ceremony would start at 4 A.M. Cairo time. Morsi's interview was supposed to air at 8 P.M. Word was out that he had made so many gaffes that the interview had to be edited and re-edited, which kept people waiting until it actually aired after midnight and very close to the airtime of the Oscars. We came up with the idea that Morsi wanted to compete with the viewership of the Oscars and made a whole Oscar-themed episode. Every time he would say something that was untrue, like listing false achievements of the government or any other bullshit rhetoric, I would appear after each video clip to give him an Oscar. One for best actor, best writer, best fiction, best liar, etc.

The interrogator recited the script to me (there was no video, remember?) and asked, "What did you mean when you said, 'Oscar best actor, Oscar best director, etc.'?"

I tried explaining the idea of the Oscars ceremony and how we tried to draw similarities between the two television events.

His next question blew my mind. "What are the Oscars?"

"Excuse me?" I said in disbelief.

"What are the Oscars? Why do you consistently refer to them in the episode?"

It took me a bit of time to realize that he was not joking. Even the younger attorneys in the room from the general prosecutor's office were stifling their giggles.

So for the next ten minutes I proceeded to try to explain what the Oscars were. After I finished he said, "So why is this funny?"

I have to say I was deeply hurt. My comedy was not appealing to him. However, trying to appeal to the humor of a man who had no point of cultural reference would have been damn near impossible. Perhaps a fart joke would have been the common denominator.

We continued with one question after the other and one accusation after the other. I continued to play dumb, denying that I was making fun of the president. But then the prosecutor asked me, "If this was not an insult, why are the people in the theater laughing?"

"I don't know, I guess you need to go and ask them," I answered with a smile.

This went on for six hours. Six hours of questioning my jokes and my puns. The mental gymnastics that I had to go through were excruciating.

At the end of all of this I was released on bail. In the days that followed everyone who was involved in those episodes—the producers, the owner of the channel, everyone—were all brought in to be questioned. Two days later, I did my show—re-creating all the events that led to my interrogation, including the major fiasco outside the courthouse. The joke was turned against the regime; I made a total fool out of them. Even Jon Stewart came to my defense and made a segment about this on his show.

What was really interesting, though, were the different reactions of the Islamists and the liberal media. The Islamists were asking for my head, and called for the permanent banning of my show. When I say they were "asking for my head," I literally mean that. In the Arab world people are used to calling in to religious programs to ask for fatwas in all aspects of life. This could range from asking whether it is okay to put your money in a Western infidel bank to praying before going to the bathroom to, wait for it, whether it is haram to have a threesome with your two wives. Yes, those were actual questions on religious shows. But you can also ask if you can kill someone or not. That happened with me. A famous sheikh went on television saying that many people had called in and emailed him asking "if it is okay to kill Bassem Youssef." What? Who asks for this shit? Instead of denouncing this, the sheikh responded, "And I told them not now."

Others went on their shows claiming that I was originally an Israeli planted in Egypt by the Mossad. I guess that earlier talk about us being an almost-Jewish family is not too far from the truth. That of course went along with other ridiculous claims, such as me being part of the Freemasons and following the thirteenth and seventeenth protocols of the Elders of Zion. Whatever the hell that means. Also, why not the fourteenth and eighteenth protocols? Not good enough? This might sound funny and absurd, but the matter of the fact is, Egypt and the rest of the Islamic world has a history of writers, artists, and even cartoonists slaughtered by angry, jealous Muslims who acted upon a fatwa or religious incitement of hate. So you can imagine the state my wife and my parents were in.

Meanwhile, the liberal media were up in arms defending my program.

Less than eighteen months later, the Islamists who called for banning me were banned themselves under the same "rule of law."

The "liberals" turned a blind eye as my program was eventually banned. Some of them even blessed the ban.

It's funny (not ha-ha funny, but funny-sad) how principles and morals could be tailored as needed. I was there. I saw it happen firsthand. I saw people calling for my freedom but later celebrating when I was shut down.

Those who called themselves liberals proved later that being well dressed, eloquent, and standing up against Islamist fascism doesn't really mean you are a liberal. On the day of my interrogation the joke was on the Islamists. But a year later the liberals were the new joke that kept on giving.

IT'S ALL DOWNHILL FROM HERE

Around March 2013 a movement sprung up out of nowhere called Tamarod, which in Arabic means "rebellion." It appeared first as a grassroots movement, which called for Morsi to step down and for new elections to follow. These protestors demanded the constitution be rewritten and to have everyone included in writing it. The movement gave Morsi until June 30, 2013, to respond to their demands. As expected, the Islamist media lashed out. The Islamists were becoming too predictable, with their usual rhetoric and accusations of this movement being funded by the usual suspects—the Coptic Christian church, America, Israel, etc.

Morsi continued to marginalize anyone from a non-Islamic background. The Muslim Brotherhood were putting their own people everywhere. The Islamization of the state was swiftly under way. My brother worked for an oil company owned by the government. He told me that during that time Muslim Brotherhood members with no experience, talent, or skills were getting hired in all positions within the company. He said that once during a lunch hour, one of his colleagues, a Muslim Brotherhood member who had been promoted for no apparent reason, was standing with him outside the company building. He looked up and said, "In a matter of months this godforsaken company will be under control." When my brother asked him what they were going to do with the army and the police and how they were going to control them, he answered, "No, that will take a couple of years, but eventually it will happen."

This pattern was repeated with many different companies and mosques. The same arrogance I saw when I met al-Shater was materializing on the ground.

When you ask Egyptians about why they hated the Muslim Brotherhood enough to turn a blind eye to all the injustice and killing that happened to the Brotherhood after they were removed from power (more on that coming up), many would tell you that the Brotherhood would have done the same to us. It was more of a feeling of *those people are coming to dominate us and use relgion to enslave us.* Many women will tell you about how they were walking in the streets and bearded men or veiled women would shout at them, "It's our country now and all of you will be covered soon." It's like when Trump supporters started cursing at people and telling them they will be deported after Trump won the election. It's like when that guy got up on a Delta flight and shouted at everybody, "Trump is your president, all of you Hillary bitches."

It doesn't matter that these were isolated incidents or that the president didn't officially endorse them. A certain atmosphere was created, and people can see the direct link to authority.

The Brotherhood had a talent of finding more and more ways to make themselves unlikable. They were like that younger obnoxious sibling who, when you tell him to leave you alone, sticks his finger as close as humanly possible to your face and proclaims, "I'm not touching you!" The Brotherhood was hated, and the worst thing they could possibly do would be to go further to the right to spite everyone. Yet that's exactly what Morsi did. He called for a huge rally, where he gathered his supporters in the biggest sports arena in Cairo. The context for the rally was supporting people in war-torn Syria, but what we saw was different. Thousands and thousands of

President Morsi supporters with banners calling for jihad, singing songs calling for jihad, and wearing green headbands, screamed that they were ready for jihad. During the speeches the thin line between jihad in Syria and jihad in Egypt disappeared. The insinuations, the references, slowly shifted from fighting God's enemies in Syria to fighting them here in Egypt.

This looked like a heavy metal concert that had gone horribly wrong.

Even worse, Morsi sat right smack in the middle of the most right-wing, bigoted Salafi sheikhs. It was the first time that he had associated himself openly with those people in a political setting. One sheikh after another came up to the podium to give his best hate speech. It was just short of a witch-hunt party; they asked the almighty Allah to curse and strike down those planning to demonstrate on June 30. This happened while the jihad-crazed crowd cheered and the president sat there awfully silent.

Whatever attempts the Muslim Brotherhood made for over a year to convince us that they were the acceptable "light" version of political Islam went down the drain on that day. We had so much hate going around that dissing the anti-Muslim people was not enough. So they had to bring in other people to hate and call for their death just for the fuck of it. In front of everyone, including the president, a famous sheikh demanded that no Shiites be admitted into Egypt, just as relations with Iran were starting to get closer.

Wait, what?

The Salafi sheikhs sure love to spread the hate around. They hate Christians, Jews, liberals, other Muslim Sunni (whom they consider to be less pious), and they still have some leftover hate to go around for Shiites. At this point, you are probably hitting Muslim info overload and are having a hard time understanding the hate between the Sunni and Shiites.

In a nutshell, think of the Red Sox and the Yankees; now give each of them a country (Saudi Arabia and Iran); now give both of them a good amount of oil, loads of money, absolute rule by their religions, lots of weapons, hateful ideology that crosses borders, and add to that a feud that originated fifteen hundred years ago over who should be the successor of the Prophet Muhammad. That should be good enough.

We have very few Shiites in Egypt, but they're just another minority that the extreme Sunni sheikhs (who are openly funded by the Saudis) love to shit on. So a few days after that lovely speech against Shiites, calling them "filth and unholy," five Shiites were killed in a remote village in Egypt. I wondered, if five people were killed as a result of direct incitement of hate in a speech, what will happen to the rest of us, who oppose the Islamist regime? Would killing us be any more difficult?

Here we had a direct sectarian speech full of violent rhetoric that would rival a Nazi party rally openly calling for a Holocaust on anyone who opposed the president. If they could incite enough hate against a minority to have them killed a few days later, what would happen to the rest of the people they incited hate against if these people openly protested the dictatorship? The Brotherhood had used their militias before, they could use them again.

As June 30 approached, it was difficult to stay hopeful. And yet, something amazing occurred that made me believe there was some good in the world. No, we didn't all suddenly get along with glitter parades in the streets and cupcakes and lollipops for everyone. However, it was the second-best thing to that: Jon Stewart came to Egypt!

JON VERSUS THE PYRAMIDS

By now you probably recognize that I am beyond just a groupie fan girl for Jon Stewart. People usually are obsessed with rock stars, models, and actors like Matthew McConaughey (well, at least before that weird car commercial), and not often a short Jewish satirist from New Jersey, but it was because of him that I started my own show and had my own theater (well, it was a rental, but that's beside the point). I had been on his show twice already and he had written an article about me for *Time* magazine when I was chosen as one of the "100 Most Influential People in the World." What more could I ask for? Well, other than having him on the show.

This dream came true when Jon was shooting his movie *Rosewater* in neighboring Jordan. He agreed to come on the show the last week of our season, two days before June 30.

Leading up to that day, things were very uncomfortable in Egypt—the countdown to the thirtieth had left the country heated and threatening to boil over. What if all hell broke loose when he was here and I couldn't get him out of Egypt? His fans and Comedy Central would kill me.

I sent Jon an email I never thought I would've had to write: "Jon, I am sorry but the twenty-eighth is too close to a very heated and unpredictable day. I don't think I can guarantee your safety."

I hit *send* and just kept kicking myself over and over. Fuck politics, really. Why couldn't we just get along long enough for Jon to visit and happily kill each other after he left?

Jon replied with one sentence, "How about I come the week before?"

That was in two days! Seriously? A new definition for awesomeness *should be added in Webster's and this guy's photo should be next to it.*

Of course I agreed. I had to cancel an interview with a famous politician to talk about the coming events, but you know what? Who cared? Not me!

So Jon made it to Egypt. Abbas arranged for a private security company to escort him, and Amr made sure that the police and secret service were involved. He was accompanied by bodyguards whose necks were as thick as his torso. When he arrived at the theater the entire street was on lockdown. Bystanders were curious if Morsi had agreed to come on the show, but then this short white guy with a long white beard (he was in movie-shooting mode) got out of the car. It was difficult for them to get a good look at him as he was overshadowed by the huge bodies all dressed in black towering over him.

I hadn't told my researchers. Only a close circle of people around me knew.

When Jon entered the editing room, everyone screamed, and the girls almost threw their panties on the imaginary stage. (More conservative women in my team considered throwing their hijabs.)

"It seemed I am loved here more than New York," Jon said. "I should consider moving here."

I took him for a tour around the theater. I felt like a proud student showing my teacher my science project.

"This theater kicks ass," he said.

He entered my office and noticed the posters with some of his quotes, like "I am not going to censor myself to comfort your ignorance." He looked at them and just said "niiiiice" in classic Stewart style.

We sat down and prepared for his appearance on the show. We thought that his entrance should be totally different from what we usually did. When the moment came, I announced, in classic propaganda style, that we had captured a foreign spy who was planning to commit crimes against the nation. Jon was escorted onto the stage wearing a black sack over his head à la Abu Gharib prison chic.

The moment I removed the sack off his head the theater erupted in screams, laughter, and cheers. I actually think there were real panties thrown on the stage this time. The applause went on for nearly two minutes. I wasn't the only Egyptian infatuated with this man!

Jon was incredible. He actually learned some dirty words in Arabic and shared them on-air; the audience ate it up. What was amazing about this interview was how we openly spoke about satire, power, and politics. He said something that still resonates with the people in Egypt: "If your regime can't take a joke, you don't have a regime."

This sentence went viral all over the region. Jon never imagined that he, an American Jew, would be welcomed in the heart of Cairo and have his quotes resonate with everyone. It was a moment where people from different cultures connected; comedy and laughter against tyranny seemed to unite us, if only briefly.

Naturally, the Islamists attacked me in their media. "He is getting an American Jew to support him before the thirtieth of June" was the common sentiment. They even analyzed some of the jokes we cracked as "Masonic signals that have evil intentions about Jews coming back to Egypt and taking over." Yup, that kind of crazy.

But all that didn't matter. This was not just my idol coming to my show.

It was validation.

I remember joking with my staff after his visit, saying: "Well, we can't top that, people; maybe it is time to shut down the show and retire."

Careful what you wish for.

LAUGHING OUR WAY TO DISASTER

Only a few days before the awaited June 30 protests, President Morsi announced that he was going to make an important speech. Morsi was like our own George W. Bush. He never failed to provide the show with the best material.

With everything happening in the country this might have been his most important speech to date. Hoping (for absolutely selfish reasons, like having a good show) he would really screw it up, we all gathered in our theater to watch it live. It was like we were watching a predictable sitcom where people laughed and cheered at every calculated punch line. The speech was a total disaster. It sounded like one given in a minor banana republic, where you'd have renegade warriors shouting and cursing American imperialism, "global conspiracies," and some made-up enemy. But Morsi's weren't made-up enemies; he was actually naming names—journalists, other media people, dissenters, etc. He stood there saying that, as the president of Egypt and as the supreme leader of the Egyptian army, he demanded respect, and that an insult to him was an insult to the entire country. The writers and the producers looked at me and clapped. I had made it into the presidential speech!

The guy had clearly lost his mind. He was adopting a sort of demagogic rhetoric that I heard only in movies. Here was a man who made the Emperor from the *Star Wars* franchise sound like a pansy.

The arena was filled with the Muslim Brotherhood youth cheering his every word, just as previously people had cheered during Mubarak's speeches, Saddam's speeches, and all the way back to the 1930s, when they'd cheered the propagandist films of Leni Riefenstahl. Morsi announced that he had commissioned the minister of youth to start summer camps for more than a million young individuals under the supervision of the government. Call me paranoid, but the way the Muslim Brotherhood "supervised" the young in the streets during protests was hardly confidence boosting in terms of how they might "supervise" a million young men in summer camps. Whether they employed violence or brainwashing to do so, the outcome, I imagined, wouldn't be too appealing. Morsi's plan echoed similar initiatives with youths in countries like Iran, where the ayatollah indoctrinated millions of young enthusiastic citizens to defend his ideologies.

Morsi didn't forget to kiss up to the army and the police. Right there in the front row was the minister of interior, aka "the Butcher," who had far too many kills under his belt and was hailed by the Muslim Brotherhood members as someone who was "protecting the legitimacy" of the presidency with his brutal powers.

Next to him was the guy who would lead to big changes very soon. His name was General Abdel Fattah al-Sissi, the minister of defense. *Remember that name.* Sissi. (Pronounced "see-see," not like the "sissy" that he is.)

Morsi praised both of these men, as if he were saying, *I am about to come down on everyone, but at least I've got you on my side, right?*

A few days later the minister of interior and Sissi would kill many of the young people sitting in that very arena, cheering for Morsi to kill his opponents.

For weeks, the Islamist newspapers published headlines hailing Morsi for deploying army troops in major cities. "The army is performing its sacred duty to protect the president and his legitimacy," they said.

The anti-Islamic channels were hysterical because the "naming game" was at McCarthy-era levels. There were rumors about a list of media figures and politicians to be arrested once the thirtieth of June came and the alleged revolution failed. I was later told by people who were investigating the Brotherhood movement that I was the second name on the list. That made me a bit jealous. Why second? What would I have to do to beat out whoever was first?

Rumors aside, what happened as we were preparing for the episode was real: we had warnings from the Muslim Brotherhood government and the media authorities controlled by them that any sarcasm directed toward the president would be dealt with swiftly and that "any channel hosting a show that would air such material would be closed down immediately." Well, that's comforting!

After a very long night of editing and writing we managed to make the airing time. We were all half asleep, but had written one of our best episodes yet. But what really stayed with our audience is how the show ended, when we actually used Morsi's own words. In his speech he had gone on complaining and whining about how certain people and "powers" were abusing democracy and attacking the presidency. He wanted everyone to know that he had been patient for a very long time, for a whole year, even, but now, "one year is enough." Did he just put a cap on democracy in this country? *Okay, guys, enough fun and games, free speech is out.* I ended the episode by saying, "You are right, Mr. President, one year is enough," implying that *his time* as president should come to an end.

I had just put myself in direct confrontation with the authorities.

As I was getting questions from the audience during the commercial break, I was asked the same exact question I was asked in all my interviews during that time: "What do you think will happen on the thirtieth of June?" I said that I really didn't know but I was worried more about what would happen *after* the thirtieth of June. Islamists had made it very difficult for anyone to work with them. And moreover, to them, the thirtieth of June was more of a survival issue. There was no compromise: I was afraid that if they continued to be in power after that date it would prove that all the efforts of the liberal forces meant nothing and they could comfortably crush whoever stood in their way. This was not a mere assumption. The disastrous "jihad" rally that Morsi attended in the stadium was a big clue of what kind of craziness could occur.

It wasn't a laughing matter anymore; the shit was just about to get real. And in a few days we would all get to know what surprises were waiting for the whole country.

A COUP WITH POPULAR DEMAND

There are so many ways to tell the story of how the Islamists lost control of the government and the military took over. But let's just start by saying traffic got much, much worse.

Millions of people who all hated each other took to the streets. The Islamists occupied a spot in eastern Cairo and threatened that if anyone came close to Morsi, they would be "wiped out."

And the rest of the country went out by the millions to call for Morsi to step down. Even if everyone knew that protests and rallies didn't mean shit.

Remember Sissi? The minister of defense whom Morsi was kissing up to just a few days earlier? Yeah, funny story, the kissing up didn't work. Sissi announced Morsi's removal on television.

This was just typical Muslim Brotherhood routine: kissing up to authority and eventually getting screwed by it.

To add insult to injury, he had representatives from all sects of the Egyptian people, including the head of the Salafi Al Nour party, stand up on-air to show their support of the removal. This was a plot twist that was on the same level as the "Red Wedding" episode in

Game of Thrones, where your closest allies stab you in the back in the most unexpected ways.

This was just typical Salafi routine, proving once again that they were nothing but tools of whichever regime was "winning." The prophecy I gave to al-Shater was fulfilled; their majority didn't last and their own allies were turning against them. Morsi and his aides were removed to an unknown location and all of the Islamist channels were shut down.

There were celebrations everywhere as people rejoiced at the removal of Morsi. Wearing sunglasses and a baseball cap, I decided to go down and mingle with the protestors around the presidential palace. There, I heard songs from my show coming from the speakers. All the songs that were made to oppose and make fun of the Muslim Brotherhood were playing in the streets and people were singing and dancing to them!

It only took one person to recognize me to start an uproar. "Bassem Youssef!" he shouted. I tried to shush him up but it was too late. Dozens of people swarmed me. My eyes were blinded with camera flashes and my face was covered with saliva from all the kisses. Yes, we Arabs like to kiss a lot, but not one of them was from a girl, damn it!

It took a miracle for me to free myself from that loving mob. I can't remember how I got home, and even though I was exhausted I was excited and happy. Yet, only a few months later, many of those same people would burn my pictures in the streets.

In eastern Cairo, the mood was not that festive. The sheikhs and the Islamists started a sit-in after days of praising the army. The banners that were calling America evil and imperialist in Arabic flipped overnight into posters in English asking Obama to interfere and reinstate Morsi. Islamist sheikhs shouted from the stage of the sit-in that the American Sixth Fleet is moving toward Egypt to liberate Morsi!

The non-Islamist channels—you know, those who were supposed to be liberal and secular—took over the role of the fascist Islamist channels and became fascist themselves. They called for wiping out the Islamists completely. The Islamists' sit-in gave the liberals the fuel they needed to spread hate. Their sit-in was televised on Al Jazeera, and the people who took to the stage were a source of awe and terror at the same time. If they were not inciting hate or calling for people to go to jihad to defend Morsi or threatening to blow things up, they were telling their thousands of followers that some sheikh dreamed the Archangel Gabriel would descend from heaven and fight alongside them. How can anyone lose when the angels are on their side?

The sit-in spurred the Islamists to violently rally and kill people who were not on "God's side." The pro-military media incited more hate, and anyone with a beard that looked remotely "Islamic" was either harassed, arrested, or killed. As if accusations of terrorism and treason were not enough, the sex card was again used. There were "repenting witnesses" coming on national television describing how "jihad fornication" was practiced. In short, this meant that women would willingly offer themselves to the mujahideen at the sit-ins as an act of jihad. This was of course bullshit, but you even had highly educated people believing the "liberal media" when it told them that the Islamists were hiding Scud missiles in their tents. They would believe anything. When I came to America two years later and interviewed Trump supporters who believed that Obama was supervising ISIS training camps in America, I saw how fear mixed with stupidity can make you believe anything. Stupid is stupid no matter what country you're from.

The hysteria had to end badly. And it did. Churches were burned, people were killed in the streets from both sides, and in one day alone around one thousand people were killed while dispersing from the Islamist sit-in. It was a massacre performed by the same police whom the Islamists had called upon before to wipe out their "liberal" enemies, and all of that happened under the watchful eye of the man himself, Sissi, with the military backing him all the way. The tables sure had turned.

Each Egyptian home was split between family members who cheered for the killings and others who vehemently opposed what was happening. Even within my own family I was viewed as unpatriotic for not fully supporting "our army."

When Morsi was removed, most people, including me, were happy. They thought the army was going to host new elections and write a new constitution. The army had no intentions of ruling, Sissi had told us so. God, we were stupid. After the killings, the violence, and martial law, the army was not acting like a dad choosing sides anymore. The army was back and this time it was here to stay.

MOMMY ISSUES

There is too much infatuation with the idea that satire can make a difference, that satirists and comedians can change the way people think, that they can speak truth to power through comedy and use humor to trump fear. This is basically how we satirists sell ourselves. This is how we get invited as keynote speakers at prestigious events, get hosted on popular TV shows, and get to write books, like this one. But the truth is, sometimes we can't even sell our cause to the people nearest to us.

When that crazy shift from being a doctor to being a satirist happened to me, my mom didn't mind me giving up medicine as long as I would be close to her in Egypt instead of leaving for Cleveland. Middle Eastern moms like to have their friends close and their kids closer. I think many mothers are secretly mob bosses: *I gave him an offer he couldn't refuse.*

She was happy with my webisodes, and she even asked me to teach her how to log on to the Internet so she could watch my YouTube videos. That was my first mistake. She didn't understand the concept of Internet trolling. She didn't understand why strangers would curse her (of course, indirectly; they were trying to insult me by cursing my mom) and she would make a huge deal out of it. But what was worse than taking those insults personally was that she took my political message personally. People always tell me that they were sure my mom was proud of me and what I did. I am sure deep inside she *was* proud of me, but that was always suppressed by the unrelenting anxiety she had because, as you know, as moms tend to do, they worry about us.

My mom belonged to an older generation who lived for decades under military dictatorship. That generation despised authority and yet couldn't imagine living any other way. It was like they were in an advanced state of Stockholm syndrome. Armies in the Arab world managed to push this narrative of "all or none." We either rule absolutely or there will be no one to protect you.

During the reign of the Muslim Brotherhood, my mom worried about me criticizing the Islamic authorities—not out of conviction but out of fear that those people would use religion to hurt me. She would spend half her time going through their Facebook pages to see how their activists were calling for killing me because I was an apostate and anti-Islamic. Telling her they were just trolls didn't manage to make her feel any better. Every time an episode of mine was broadcast, I had to worry about two things: (1) Did people like it? and (2) Did my mom have a panic attack because of its political content? More often than not, people liked it *and* my mom had a panic attack.

Both my parents fell victim to the lies of the pro-military media before they became a coup. They became avid followers of our own versions of *Fox and Friends*. They surrendered their brains to the same vicious propaganda machine that I was working diligently to fight. They would watch my show, laugh, worry about me, and then when I visited them at home they would sit there in front of the same brainwashing media that I made fun of. They succumbed to the fear-mongering of talking heads and yet continued to laugh at them when I made fun of them on my show. My mom warned me that she would disown me if I dared to talk against the military. My mom was living proof that Egyptians held the military as holier than religion. To her, criticizing the army was a blasphemous act.

This military worship isn't too dissimilar from when people in the States were called anti-American for disagreeing with the Iraqi War. Super-nationalists would label those who disliked the war as anti-military. And if Americans criticized the war, they were also seen as criticizing "our fine men and women in uniform who protect our country," and they were told they should get the fuck out because they weren't true Americans. Thankfully for you, American soldiers have yet to turn against their own country, but now you may have some perspective on how upsetting and frightening it would be if they did.

Well, back to my mother. Like many Egyptians, she hated Mubarak and she hated the military coup that brought Nasser to power in the 1950s. She somehow managed to separate those leaders and the damage they did to the country from the fact that they came from the army. As if the military were made of gnomes rather than officers, and those gnomes eventually became the dictators they pledged to hate.

When I started to protest the military crimes committed against the protestors after the coup, I would receive angry calls from my mom. We would fight on the phone every single time. This wasn't an uncommon occurrence—the same thing was happening in all of my friends' families. There was a huge disconnect between us and our parents' generation. The fights often turned ugly. Many of them ended with families broken over political differences. It's like a liberal college kid living with his racist dad. Nothing good comes out of this.

Martial law was enforced after the coup, so for a few weeks I couldn't go back on-air. I loathed the day of my return, not just because of the dilemma I would be in by having to make fun of a very shitty situation, but also because I feared my mom's reaction. If she was angered by my opinions in a normal conversation, how would she react to my satirical show now?

My career had already become a burden on my very patient wife. But now it was alienating many members of my family, especially the elderly, especially my mom. It got to the point where she and I just stopped talking to each other.

After more than two weeks of phone boycott, I gave her a call. It was a ten-minute call with nothing but small talk. We talked about the tree she'd planted by herself in her garden and how it suffered because of the strong wind the day before. We talked about mundane things like what she had cooked that day. We talked about my daughter, Nadia, whom I named after her as a not so secret way of earning her hard to receive approval. We talked about everything but politics. I tried hard to avoid that topic.

My show had been suspended two months earlier because of curfew enforced by the army. There was too much violence in the streets and no way to continue doing the show at that point. Maybe this was better. Maybe that reduced friction between my mom and me. I hung up with my mom, wondering what would happen to her when my show returned, *if* it returned. Knowing her and knowing how inflammatory she could get, I was truly worried what it would do to her, especially given her chronic high blood pressure.

The very next day after that call, I received a call from Dad.

My mom had died.

She went peacefully in her sleep. She didn't suffer, she didn't go through a long painful death like her own mother had, a fate she dreaded all her life. How peaceful for her and utterly devastating for us.

I only have memories of a strong and defiant mom. I recognize that not everyone can say this about their mother and I see this as a blessing. She was spared the humiliation of health deterioration and was saved from the agony of living in a country that would later persecute her son. I was spared the guilt I would have had every time my show would air, putting more pressure on our relationship. Her departure liberated her. Her absence liberated me. She was my strength, my weakness, and the only reason I would excel in something was just to make her proud of me. Even if she hid her pride under her constant worry.

I was alone in this now. Nothing really mattered after her. Even if you have your own family, when Mom is gone, she leaves a void that can never be filled. At the funeral service my dad sat next to me. He was a much more easygoing parent. He didn't concern himself too much with what I would say on my show as long as he got his weekly free tickets. As a retired judge, that was his way to brag in front of his friends, that he could get them the hottest ticket in town. "This sadness will pass," he told me. "You need to figure out what you want to do. I don't envy you. Whether you choose to go back or not is up to you and I will support your decision, whatever it may be."

I hugged him and promised that I would make him proud.

"Just make sure when you come back," he added, "that you get me a couple of extra tickets every week. I have a few friends I owe a few favors to!"

Leave it to a satirist's dad to make a sly joke at a funeral.

I didn't know if I should go back on-air. With all that was happening, the thought of making fun of the new regime seemed suicidal. What should I do? I needed to ask the only person that might have the answer.

PART THREE

THE CLOWN, THE TRAITOR, THE OUTCAST

W.W.J.D.? (WHAT WOULD JON DO?)

Our supporters would praise me, and in the streets fans would come and greet me, as the man who stood against the Muslim Brotherhood. "You had a big role in this revolution," they would tell me. "If it wasn't for you and your show, people would not have figured them out. You showed us their true side."

Many of the older generation would greet me and then slam me with a precautionary warning: "Now, don't go and do the same to Sissi. He is different."

I didn't like that some people thought of me as a mercenary who would cherry-pick whom I used my satire on. The fact that I was an equal opportunity offender was lost on people. They liked satire as long as it was on their side.

I was a regular contributor to a weekly column in a popular newspaper called *Al Shorouk*. I wrote an article warning people that we were replacing religious fascism with nationalistic fascism. I was so naive to think that writing about love and coexistence, and learning from those who'd made hatred and extremism their way of life, would make people wake up and accept basic human values. You know, like being human. But people were just too angry and too on edge to accept reason, let alone satire. We were living our own version of the Roman Coliseum, where the only shout that was welcomed was "Kill, kill, kill."

I called for a meeting with everyone involved in the show—Tarek, Amr, and the board governing our production company.

I was under so much stress trying to decide what to do next. How could I come back on-air? What could I make fun of? I couldn't make fun of the Muslim Brotherhood anymore; they were either jailed or dead. And I would be screwed over if I remotely touched those in power now. I couldn't even label what had happened as a coup, not even jokingly.

So I made my mind up and told them I wanted out. I didn't want to do the show anymore. Many of the people who were waiting for the show's return were not waiting for it as fans; they were waiting to crucify me if I said something they didn't like.

Can you imagine a guy trying to have a political satire show in the time of Mussolini? Well, I was that idiot.

Naturally, everybody opposed my decision to retire. We had a contract with the channel. The show was the flagship product of the company and if I stopped, hundreds of people would lose their jobs. So I asked for some time to think. I went home that night and wrote an email to Jon Stewart. He was still in Jordan shooting his movie *Rosewater*.

"I am in deep shit, I don't know what to do and I need to see you," I wrote.

Jon was following the news and was checking on me regularly. He knew what I was going through. He told me to hop on the first plane to Jordan to have a chat.

Of course, I did just that. I landed in Amman, happy to see my friend. I filled him in on everything that was happening back home. He was horrified. Even he suggested that I just quit. I told him that too many people were depending on me. So he sat there silently for a while and then said, "Listen, not to compare here, but I might have gone through a similar experience. It was not an experience where we had a military regime or anything, but that whole 'we are in a state of war' mentality was there. Right after 9/11 we didn't know what to do. We didn't know what to make fun of. Everything was too sensitive, every joke sounded politically incorrect. People were scared. People were confused. So we decided to write exactly what we felt. People were afraid and that was the general mode. So we made fun about the fact that we can't make fun of that. We made fun of the fact that we were afraid to joke about anything. Maybe this could work for you. You guys are afraid of talking about the current regime so just write what you feel. If you feel the big guy is untouchable, make fun of that. Write what you feel and you will find out that the people who watch you are humans like you. They will connect, they will relate. When we tried that we were surprised that people laughed from the bottom of their hearts. They needed that, you could feel it. Your sarcasm can actually be the tool that heals the country."

Well, shit, Jon, when you say it like that!

I asked him about the fans. I said, "There are too many people who expect a certain, directed kind of sarcasm. I feel they want me to continue making fun of people who are no longer in power. I can't do that. It is not right. I am afraid that I will lose a lot of my fans. A lot of people will hate me when they see I went against them."

"Well, yes, that might happen," he replied. "So tell me, what else are you afraid of? Your safety? That they might jail you? What? What is your biggest fear?"

I thought about it for a minute and said, "Well, if they put me in jail that will make them look too stupid."

"I agree," he said.

"I guess it is just the fact that I might lose the popularity and the support," I finally admitted.

"Well, my friend," he said, "that is true courage. Standing up for what you believe might not be what the people want. You're staying true to yourself no matter what the consequences are, though . . . that is true integrity. Bassem, remember when I visited you in Egypt? I told you that you need to ask yourself, what do you want to do? Do you want to do comedy? Or do you want to do something that lasts longer? When you answer that, you will know what to do."

"Dude, you never fail to impress me," I said.

"Well, I am not in your shoes, and I can't imagine being in your position. We sometimes take freedom of speech for granted in the U.S. It is people like you that will have to carve out their own space. Whether you succeed or you fail, you have already made your mark in history."

I realized how far I had come in only two years. And here was my idol cheering me on. His words echoed in my head: "Write what you really feel, you will find a way. If you are afraid, make fun of your fear. If you can't speak, make fun of that."

We hugged, bid each other farewell, and then I made my way back to Cairo, determined to follow his advice. I was worried that I would be screwed because of it.

I was right.

A LONG-AWAITED VISIT

"We are doing this," I said to my partners in the company. "We're going ahead with the show."

They were thrilled that I would be back but as they wished me good luck I saw the look of *here goes a dead man walking* in their eyes. The hysteria in Egypt was just unbearable. No one could speak against the regime and they expected me to make fun of it? This sucked big-time.

Many of my "liberal" friends turned fascist overnight and actually believed the bullshit the military was pushing. There is something very interesting about becoming a fascist. It turns you instantly into a dumbass. The same educated people who'd traveled the world and called for freedom and liberalism and opposed the fascist agenda of the Islamists had now turned into what they were attacking for the past couple of years.

Egyptians who'd lived for decades in the United States believed that America was conspiring against Egypt because they had initially objected to the removal of Morsi by the military. Don't worry, though, they still honorably paid taxes to the federal government that was conspiring against their motherland in a classic example of "double think."

Egypt was now living out a George Orwellian reality; it was as if we were living inside the pages of a poorly written *1984*.

After four months of enforced curfew, we came back to the theater to prepare for our return.

The first meeting with my team was different from anything we'd had before. It revealed how schizophrenic our society had become. All of the members of my team came from homes where their parents had turned into pro-military fascists. Anything less than absolute support for the army, absolute love of Sissi, and absolute hate against anyone else was unacceptable. Some of my young producers and researchers were having trouble coming back to the show because their parents were forbidding them to speak against Sissi. There was clearly a generation gap. Their parents were the ones who'd lived under the persecution of Nasser and knew firsthand what living under a military dictatorship looked like. Now the same people were supporting the same model of the benevolent military dictator. One would think that they would have learned something from their life experience.

I retold Stewart's advice about just writing what we felt. If we felt that we were afraid or had nothing to say, we should talk about that. We should all expect that we would lose a lot of our popularity but at least we would be true to ourselves. They understood my message and were on board.

With only four days left till our comeback, I received a call from a number I didn't recognize. I didn't reply at first but then checked the number against a caller ID service. It gave me the name "Muhamed Mukhabarat." For the record *Mukhabarat* in Arabic means "intelligence." This was like seeing "Mike Laundry" or "John Electrician" or "Paul FBI" or, for those who can't remember who they took home last night, "Mark Sexy Bartender" on your caller ID.

The number called again and this time I answered.

"Hello, am I speaking to Dr. Bassem Youssef?"

"Yes, sir, who is it?"

"It's Mohamed—from the General Intelligence Agency," he replied.

"Are you guys arresting me?"

He giggled on the other side. "No, no, no, we are big fans. I just want to meet you and have some coffee with you."

"It would be an honor, sir, would next week be okay?"

"Oh no, we really need to meet as soon as possible, before your comeback episode. You are coming back onscreen in two days, right?"

"You are not asking, are you? It would be a shame if you didn't know," I added jokingly.

"Oh my god, you are hilarious! Exactly like you are on TV. So tomorrow at two?"

"Of course, I will be waiting for you at the theater," I said. As if I had a choice.

At two o'clock sharp he was there. It was nice to know that these people were at least punctual. He gave me his ID card, which read GENERAL INTELLIGENCE AGENCY, HEAD OF THE COMMITTEE OF DIRECTING MEDIA. Now that's a title!

But was that actually his job? To "direct" media? There's no way he could be a true director; he wasn't even wearing a baseball cap and tennis shoes!

He knew what I was thinking because he said, "Please ignore the title. We believe in free press. We never tell people what to do or say."

"Of *course* you don't," I replied.

For the first half hour we talked about general things. He knew (of course) that I played a lot of sports, so he shared stories of his sports days too. Then I just had to cut to the chase. "Not to be rude, sir, but what do you guys want from me?"

"We are here just to get to know each other. We wanted you to know that we like your work and we will be supporting you in anything you need."

I didn't quite understand, so he continued.

"As you know, Dr. Bassem, Egypt is going through very critical times. We wanted to make sure that we would be on the same page when it comes to national security." ("Critical times" and "national security" were always used by authorities in Egypt as a polite way to tell people to *shut the fuck up*.)

"Errrr, I don't know what you mean, exactly?" I said.

"Well, we just want you to include us whenever you are going to speak about something sensitive so we would give you the best advice."

"Do you mean that you want to interfere with my content?"

"Oh, god no." He paused and then added in a low, firm voice, "But just to let you know, Sissi is very popular. I am not telling you not to make fun of him, but the masses wouldn't like that. That's all."

I understood the message. This visit had opened my eyes to how media were "directed" in Egypt. There were different levels of media faces. There were the lowlife scum who received direct orders about what to say onscreen, but for the more "prestigious" and "respected" anchors, it was different.

There was an ongoing urban legend that said that each anchor had his own liaison officer either from the army, the intelligence service, or our own version of the NSA. This officer would basically be the "close confidant" of that anchor. The two would simply have occasional "casual" conversations about what was happening in the country and the world. For the anchor, this was a great relationship to maintain, because he now had an inside scoop. For the officer, he could slowly brainwash the anchor into believing whatever he wanted him to believe.

Even if the anchor was not totally sold on the officer's stories, he would prefer to play it safe and stay on the good side of the authorities while justifying to himself that he was "serving his country."

So I wanted to test this theory with that guy. I asked him about all the bullshit conspiracies I had been hearing on television. He enthusiastically confirmed every shitty piece of "intel," and then added even more crazy stuff. So this was *my* liaison officer. I was supposed to repeat that shit on my show. It was no surprise that he stopped calling after the episode aired.

PISS THE NATION

I can't remember a time when I was more terrified, and we had been living in terrifying times. I was in my dressing room making small talk with the hairdresser and the makeup lady, but I wasn't really aware of what the hell I was saying. My mouth and tongue were making the movements while I was totally disconnected from reality.

It had been four months since I was last onstage. I didn't know what was waiting for me out there. What kind of a crowd would it be? Would there be angry people willing to boo me if I made jokes about the current regime? What were they expecting from me? Crew members passed by me all day and patted me on the back and said, "Good luck, Bassem," which, to me, sounded like *Dude, you are doomed.*

I took a few strides to the backstage area and waited. I was contemplating calling the whole thing off. Maybe I could come down with a bad case of diarrhea. Wouldn't that be a way to escape? I stood there thinking about how people would look back at my time on television: *Well, he was this hilarious guy, really good at hosting his show—but then he had one epic shit and his career was all over . . .* Thankfully it was too late for me to rewrite my destiny: I heard the credits, the opening music, and then the countdown in my earpiece. In slow motion, I took the stage and the people cheered. Then for a moment that felt like eternity, I was silent. I went with Jon's advice and decided to tell them what I felt, and by doing that I tapped into what everyone was feeling in that moment.

I went into a monologue that echoed everything that was going on in the country. Every single phrase that was running across people's lips, every fear and doubt, every suspicion and frustration that entered into our minds. I put into words the torn reality we were all living—a mishmash of conflicting emotions and opposing thoughts. It's like how you in America on any given day will throw out phrases like *minimum wage, police brutality, Black Lives Matter, Obamacare, iPhone's wireless headphones,* and *Trump is an asshole*. But my rant was the rant of a scared, terrified man. A man who was broken and not sure what to do next. That was the state of the country and people connected with it.

At that time no one was allowed to show confusion or have second thoughts. There was a set of rules you needed to follow in the media, and if you didn't you would be crushed. How could you show confusion in this time of war? The only accepted narrative was: it was a revolution—don't even think the word *coup*—and everyone is conspiring against us.

Yet I went on to joke about whether what had happened was a coup or a revolution. Questioning that at that time proved later to be very costly. The word *coup* was considered blasphemous.

For the first time we didn't make fun of the Islamists. I directed my sarcasm at the "liberal" media now. I always felt it was my job to keep whoever was in power in check—and even though these people used to root for me and against the Islamists back in the day, they were now the ones fueling hate and racism. On that night whatever friends or supporters I had in the media were lost.

The popularity of Sissi was soaring. Criticizing him was considered career suicide. People celebrated the fact that Sissi's photo was on everything: gold chains, wedding gifts, and even pants sold in the flea market. Shit, they even had his face on cupcakes and chocolates so you could bite his head off. We came up with the slogan: "A taste that is irresistible, you can't resist it, even if you wanted to, resistance is futile!" So instead of criticizing his new, god-like status, we embraced it and even asked for more. Sarcasm *is* a blessing in disguise.

The episode finally came to an end. This was one of the most intense days I had ever been through. When I went home and collapsed in my bed and tried to fall asleep, I received a very disturbing call. It was Tarek.

"They arrested my dad," he said.

One hour after we finished taping, the police had gone to his house and arrested his father on charges of "hate incitement" and "funding terrorist activities."

His father was sixty-seven with a heart condition and diabetes and he seldom left the house. Although an Islamist, he'd instructed all his family members that no one was to go to the Islamists' sit-in.

Of course the charges were a bunch of bullshit but he was detained anyway.

His lawyer told Tarek that someone in the prosecutor's office had told him that these were bullshit charges but they came from high above to pressure me.

Tarek had been living this ongoing Greek tragedy since my show started. It was not just that his dad was angry at him because of my show during the Morsi era. Tarek's brother, who joined Morsi's staff, was arrested the day they arrested Morsi. Tarek's father kicked Tarek out of the house, blaming him for what happened.

For the next year and a half, Tarek's brother and father remained in jail for no apparent reason, under no logical charge, until they were released because of health problems.

Tarek was lucky enough to be in Dubai when his father was arrested. He never came home to Egypt because he was afraid that he would be arrested just because of the association with his family. A year later I would be escaping from Egypt to join him.

THE MORNING AFTER

It was the Saturday morning after the comeback episode was aired. I went for my morning run at the Gezira Club, the upper-class venue full of army supporters I told you about. I didn't know what to expect. Twitter and social media were buzzing all night with reactions to the episode. There was a general sense of confusion. It was the first time in four months that someone in mainstream media had been anything other than a total asswipe for Sissi. Ultra-pro-Sissi people on social media didn't lash out at me yet. They were more disappointed because I hadn't just come out and made fun of the Islamists as they were used to me doing previously. They wanted me to be "more supportive of the nation as we were fighting terrorism."

On the other extreme, Islamists were attacking me because I hadn't made enough fun of Sissi.

But a good majority of the Internet comments were actually celebrating the episode. Many people were waiting to see if I would have the balls to say anything about the current regime. The hidden jokes, the insinuations, and the innuendos I'd made might be much more subtle than my "in your face" remarks during the Morsi era, but given the mass hysteria, many of those silenced by the new regime considered that episode a lifeline.

Going to the club the next day was my first encounter with the real world after the episode. People began to notice me, and many waved and flashed a thumbs-up sign. *Okay, this is going well!* People actually came over and approached me as I was warming up. "We are proud of you," they said. "We didn't expect any less of you."

I was pleasantly surprised. There were people of all ages—young, middle aged, and even a handful of older people—who came to tell me how delighted they were with the episode. However, I couldn't please everyone. Some older people in their fifties and sixties weren't very happy, and they wanted to make sure I knew it. They were still cordial, but expressed their disappointment in how "out of line" I was.

In general it was a good morning, but things were about to change.

That night, the talk-show cycle in which I was the main topic of conversation began. Many of the hosts viciously attacked me, saying that I was "insulting the army" and "insulting Egypt." The phone lines were open on many of these shows so people could freely curse me.

Over the next two days it got worse, much worse. There was nothing else in the media but people attacking me. A week later one of the programs that specialized in reviewing the press discovered an interesting statistic. In just one week there were more than 740 articles written about me and that "rogue" episode.

One article suggested that I was a "mole" planted in Egypt a long time ago. The author of the article, who was a parliament member with known ties to the army, said that I was chosen by the CIA to be trained by Jon Stewart to use satire to destroy the country! To make the story look credible, the author stated that the CIA officers were training me in a certain apartment in one of Cairo's districts, and he even gave the address of the place. That was the address of our production company! If Jon was the CIA's pick as a recruiter, America would've been in deep shit a long time ago.

It was insane. There was an elaborate spread in the pages of one popular newspaper with more than twelve articles focused just on me. Half of them ripped me apart and the rest were either mild in their defense or reminded people that I was the same guy they carried on their shoulders a few weeks ago, when my jokes were appropriate enough.

Suddenly, my jokes became a threat to the values of the "Egyptian Family." My bleeped "profanity" under the Islamist regime was celebrated as a form of resistance, but now everyone was a fucking prude. The shift in public opinion led by the obviously biased media was now becoming apparent. I went back to the club just a few days later; the same people who'd politely disagreed with me one day after the episode were more aggressive when they spoke to me now. The episode they had watched seemed to have morphed in their minds into some sick exorcism. The media were succeeding in making me out to be a monster. "You can't insult the army," they would say. I would ask them how I had insulted the army but no one could answer. It was the same thing that had happened months earlier, when pious Muslims accused me of insulting Islam but when I asked them what exactly I had said to insult Islam, they couldn't answer.

My network issued a statement distancing itself from the content of the episode. The statement said that the network couldn't be part of something that would "insult and degrade the foundations of the nation and the general manners of the public." Motherfuckers!

They basically threw me under the bus. Despite the fact that the network's owner had, during our last episode, been sitting right there in the front row, giggling, clapping, and howling at every joke.

Now the owner sent the manager of the network and one of his prominent anchors to talk with me.

"The owner wants to know if you thought the thirtieth of June a revolution or a coup," they said.

I felt that I had traveled back in time to the Spanish Inquisition. "Why is this important?" I asked.

"This is the most important issue here," they answered. "If you think it was a revolution, many of our differences could be resolved easily, but if you think it is a coup, that would be a fundamental difference."

Of course I had to say it was a revolution; at least part of me was still believing that it was at that time. But I really didn't like the fact that it had to be pressured out of me like this.

I told them that what they did issuing that statement was totally out of line. It was a stab in the back.

"Oh yes, about that, the owner doesn't want you to speak about this statement," they said.

"Hell no, you fucked me in front of the whole nation, I will be opening the next episode with that," I answered angrily.

"He will not be very happy," they said.

"Well, he knew what he was getting into when he signed me a year ago," I answered.

So . . . that didn't go very well, but things were getting even worse right outside my theater.

Protestors gathered there for the next three days. They were burning my photos; they were cursing me and my family; they were accusing me of the usual shit of being an operative and a spy.

The theater was literally under siege; we had to go in and out using a back door. These "protestors" were the same thugs we had seen since the beginning of the revolution. They were known to be "rented heads" by the intelligence service, to give a false sense that this mentality was the will of the people. We had seen these thugs in videos supporting the army on many occasions.

There were people outside the theater threatening to kill me.

They had posters of me with a large X on my face, calling me a Zionist dog. (*Why does it always have to be someone's dog?*) They were harassing anyone coming in or out of the theater. Some of them were talking to the media outside, saying that they wouldn't mind killing me and sticking a knife in my heart if they saw me because "the army was above all."

We were supposed to somehow write comedy under these conditions.

Some of my young researchers and producers were getting calls from their parents, who were pleading with them to leave the theater and come back home. Some of them had daily fights with their parents over the next few weeks as they tried to leave home to go to work.

As we sat down to write the next episode I insisted that we should start it by making fun of the statement the channel had issued. It was easy since the same channel who was now saying they cared about protecting the foundations and the manners of the "Egyptian Family," and couldn't tolerate anything that might offend the beliefs and traditions of the Egyptian people, had broadcast a Ramadan series that was full of profanity during the holiest month of the year.

We taped the episode as usual. I traveled to Dubai right after that to catch up with Tarek, who was scared to go back home after the arrest of his dad. We were out having dinner as the time came for the episode to air. My brother called me and was flipping out on the phone. The channel had issued another statement saying that it had suspended the program for the time being. My phone was ringing off the hook, with many of my friends and even celebrities asking what was going on.

This was a shock to everyone. Ours was the most successful show in the history of Arabic television. There was no way this suspension was a business decision; this came from high up the food chain.

We didn't know what to do. I returned to Egypt and set a meeting with the owner. When I met him and his lawyers, he told me that he had suspended the show to respect the will of the people.

We both knew the "people" were a handful of thugs, a bunch of expired old men and women, and the assholes in the media who prostituted themselves to any kind of authority. Will of the people, my ass!

"The country is in a critical condition now and I can't allow my channel to be part of this," the owner told me. "We are thankful for what you have done in the past; your contribution to enlighten people against Islamic fascism will not be forgotten. But Egypt doesn't need you now."

I told him I was not doing this because of a political agenda. I was doing it because it was the right thing. I couldn't be a puppet in the hands of authority to mislead the people. We were living in strange times. The people of Egypt thought they had gotten rid of fascism, but they were in denial; they had only replaced religious fascism with military fascism.

The owner tried to offer more money and better conditions under the contract to convince me to agree to his agenda. "Why not change the show a bit? Why not adopt a late-night-show format where you play games with celebrities, you know, like Jimmy Fallon? People are tired of politics now."

What he was really saying was that *they* didn't want anyone to question politics now.

Instead of me making jokes that really mattered to the people, they wanted me to become a big joke. A glorified, highly paid court jester.

I couldn't do it.

I left the meeting with the owner's words echoing in my head: "Egypt doesn't need you anymore."

BETWEEN TWO NETWORKS

For the following four months I was unemployed while my team and I took our case to arbitration against the channel.

We were already drowning in legal and financial problems. We were renting the theater out of our own pockets and still had to pay salaries for the researchers, writers, and employees.

We had to find a new channel, and fast.

In the meanwhile I was chosen to receive an award from the Committee to Protect Journalists (CPJ), one of the most prestigious awards given to journalists all around the world. The only problem was I was not a journalist. I thought I should just go to New York and get the award before anyone would notice.

The beautiful surprise was that Jon Stewart would be the one handing me the award. Big brother, always there for me.

I traveled to New York with my dad. We both needed this after my mother's death. And since my show was off the air and I didn't have free tickets to give him, I offered him tickets to New York instead! My dad didn't speak English too well. He didn't even try to speak it because he was too proud to show that he was not fluent. But on that night of the awards ceremony, he was happy and very proud of me; his smile spoke louder than words.

Jon Stewart gave a moving speech: "Me and Bassem have the

same job, but Bassem works under a totally different set of circumstances." He went on to describe what I had to go through to just say a joke. Then he delivered his best lines. "Bassem was loved and adored, millions of people followed him each night. It was amazing, there was nothing like it. When Morsi wore a hat, Bassem wore a funnier hat." He then went on to describe the new situation after the Muslim Brotherhood were toppled. "Bassem could have stopped at this moment; he was a hero. He had his name chanted to him in the streets, by all the people who called for Morsi's ouster. He could have quit right now and remain a hero, or he could stand for a higher principle; which was not that his satire was not purposeful for regime change but that his satire was purposeful for expression. So Bassem Youssef stood up and did his show and made fun of the new regime and their funny hats. And that lasted a day. So it turned out that the new regime has less of a sense of humor than the Muslim Brotherhood."

I can't even remember what I said after that in my acceptance speech. It was too touching. That son of a bitch Stewart manages to just amaze me every time.

But my speech was okay too!

I went back to Egypt to discover that finding another channel was not as easy as I thought. We were the hottest ticket in media and yet many were scared to deal with such a "toxic" brand. We were loved by the people, at least many of them, but not by the authorities. And in a country like ours, usually what the authorities want is much more important.

MBC, the biggest network in the region, pursued us. It was in seventh place overall in the ratings while CBC (the one that shut us down) was in first place. So I went ahead and signed with them. But what was interesting was that they added a clause in the article that would protect them in case the show was abruptly stopped for

THAT'S MY BRILLIANT TEAM BEHIND THE MAKING OF THE SHOW.
OH, AND IF YOU LOOK REALLY HARD, JON IS IN THERE. © *Yehia El Zeiny*

THE MIRACULOUS AIDS MACHINE. YES, IT WAS AN ATM-LIKE MACHINE
THAT WAS SUPPOSED TO HELP YOU GET RID OF AIDS, HEPATITIS C,
PSORIASIS, DIABETES, AND WHATEVER BRAIN CELLS YOU HAD LEFT.
THE PERSON DIRECTLY TO THE LEFT OF THE MACHINE, WEARING
MILITARY ATTIRE AND A CAP, IS PROF. "DR." ABDEL ATTI, A GENERAL
IN THE MEDICAL CORP. © *EgyptianTV*

**HOW IT LOOKED ON FILMING NIGHTS. CAIRO HAD NEVER SEEN
ANYTHING LIKE THIS BEFORE. ALSO, I HAVE A HUGE HEAD.**

© Sara Taksler

THE PRESS CONFERENCE WHERE I ANNOUNCED THE END
OF THE SHOW. SOME PEOPLE WERE CRYING, SOME WERE
HOLDING IT TOGETHER WITH A SMILE. I WAS ONE OF THE
LATTER. © Yehia El Zeiny

MOMENTS AFTER PROTESTORS CROSSED THE BRIDGE
INTO TAHRIR, OVERCOMING HUNDREDS OF SECURITY FORCES.
© Khaled Abo Al Naga

SEASON 6, EPISODE 9, OF *GAME OF THRONES*, ALSO KNOWN
AS THE "BATTLE OF THE BASTARDS," ALSO KNOWN AS THE
"DAY OF ANGER." THIS WAS THE ULTIMATE STANDOFF BETWEEN
THE EGYPTIAN SECURITY FORCES AND THE PROTESTORS. THE
DEFEAT OF THE BLACK-DRESSED SOLDIERS AND THE RETREAT
OF THE ARMORED VEHICLES MARKED A NEW ERA IN OUR
HISTORY. FEAR WAS DEFEATED, TILL IT CAME BACK WITH
A VENGEANCE A COUPLE OF YEARS LATER. © *Ahmed Al Masry*

THE SQUARE, THE MOST GLORIOUS MOMENT IN RECENT
EGYPTIAN HISTORY, AND THE BIGGEST TRAFFIC JAM IN
RECENT HISTORY. © Khaled Abo Al Naga

ADOLF MUBARAK, OUR THIRTY-YEAR DICTATOR, DEPICTED HERE
AS HITLER. HITLER LOOK-ALIKES EITHER ARE BOOTED OUT OF
OFFICE IN THE MIDDLE EAST OR WEAR AN ORANGE WIG AND WIN
AN ELECTION IN DEMOCRATIC FIRST WORLD COUNTRIES.

AN INTEGRAL PART OF OUR REVOLUTION WAS ENTERTAINMENT,
WHICH WAS USUALLY DEADLY. AS ONE WOULD EXPECT OF
AN ANCIENT CIVILIZATION, ATTEMPTS TO RECLAIM TAHRIR
SQUARE AFTER IT WAS TAKEN BY PROTESTORS WERE EQUALLY
ANCIENT. PRO-MUBARAK THUGS ATTACKED THE SQUARE
USING HORSEMEN AND "CAMEL MEN" USUALLY RESERVED FOR
ENTERTAINING TOURISTS AT THE PYRAMIDS. © *Ahmed Al Masry*

JON AT THE DEMOCRATIC NATIONAL CONVENTION ACCEPTING
THE NOMINATION IN 2020. I AM HIS RUNNING MATE. A JEW
AND A MUSLIM TICKET. I KNOW, IT SOUNDS RIDICULOUS.
SO WAS TRUMP. OKAY, REALLY, THIS WAS JON COMING ON TO
MY SHOW IN CAIRO. © *Yehia El Zeiny*

JON BEING INTRODUCED À LA ABU GHRAIB PRISON STYLE.
THIS IS THE HIGHEST ACHIEVEMENT OF MY CAREER, THE
VALIDATION OF MY WORK. © *Yehia El Zeiny*

reasons "out of their hands." In other words, they wouldn't have to pay a huge amount of money to me if they canceled the show because they were told to do so. Everyone was aware of the risks and expected the worst. I couldn't be very picky, though.

But now things were different. One of the first laws that was enforced by the interim government was to ban demonstrations and protests. It was weird, considering that the people in power now had come to power on the back of massive demonstrations and protests.

Droves of people, including some of my friends, were arrested for the most trivial reasons. You didn't have to go out and demonstrate; police officers were stopping people randomly in the streets, checking their cell phones to see if they had shared Facebook statuses that opposed Sissi.

Sissi's popularity was scary. He was loved, feared, revered, and coveted. Whenever you have a discussion with a person blinded by his unconditional support of the military, he will state that Sissi being popular is proof that he is the best option. The same supporter would be pissed if you mentioned other "popular" leaders. What an interesting "cool kid" lunch table that'd be: Hitler, Mussolini, Mugabe, Putin, Castro, and Kim Jong-un.

I was doing the television interview rounds to promote my long-awaited return. It had been four months since they banned me. The hosts who conducted the interviews told me, behind the scenes, how terrified they were, that they couldn't operate under the pressure, and admitted that they were hosting me because they could safely be vocal through me.

When I was asked if Sissi should be president, I said no. That was enough for them to launch a huge campaign against me in the media, calling me all kinds of names. Only a few months earlier I was the guy who'd toppled the Islamists with his jokes. Now I was accused of being not just an American operative, as I was accused during the Islamists' time, but also a covert Islamist!!! When the people making these allegations were faced with the fact that I was spearheading the attack against the Islamists making fun of them, on my show all the time, they simply stated that this was all part of a deal to vent people's anger through satire. Once you adopt a conspiracy, you can find all kinds of ways to justify anything.

These accusations were made by anchors, TV personalities, actors, and journalists who were lining up to get a statement from me and who had celebrated me when I was included in *Time*'s list of "100 Most Influential People" only a year earlier. I remember my late mother being at the *Time* party, looking at those celebrities and telling me, "The moment you say something they don't like they will turn against you." Mothers know best.

I was afraid of the influence the Saudi government would have on MBC. The idea of a totally free media in our region was now a distant memory. Now we were not debating what we would write for our next episode, but how many episodes we would last on-air.

Days before the comeback, I received an offer from *60 Minutes*, which wanted to come to Egypt to cover this period of my life. The great Bob Simon arrived to do that interview with me. I was about to get my own fifteen minutes of American fame. Meanwhile, I was getting "defamed" in my own country.

Seriously, how do you make comedy in the middle of all of this? Well, very carefully.

SHITTING MY PANTS WITH BOB SIMON

Bob Simon and the *60 Minutes* crew accompanied me while I prepared for the debut, or in this case, re-debut of the show. His questions were nothing but trouble, and I answered in a way that gave no real substance. He would ask me about military takeover, about the "coup," about the people detained, and about the people behind the scenes trying to cancel my show. I knew that if I answered those questions honestly, I would end up losing the show before it even started. When he asked me about the deterioration of human rights and the decline of democracy in Egypt, I answered, "What are you talking about? We are enjoying a *great* deal of freedom." The satirical tone was too obvious. When he asked about me giving up the "American dream" to become a surgeon for a TV show in Egypt, I told him that I was living the Egyptian dream every day.

"And what is that dream?" he asked me.

"Well, the dream of doing comedy and being called a traitor every day. *You can't beat that!*"

Bob interviewed me on the streets of Cairo. He was surprised when dozens of people stopped me to ask when I would be back on TV.

"I thought you were hated," he told me.

"Only if you follow the media and hang out with older people," I said. "The younger generation is more difficult to control. They don't have the power but they don't like what is happening. The older people can attack me twenty-four hours a day but *Albernameg* was still the most watched show in history and they can't change that. Young people don't fall for propaganda as their parents did during the Nasser era. There is Internet, YouTube, and a million other sources of information. They can't block them forever."

THE COMEBACK EPISODE ON MBC EGYPT WAS YET ANOTHER MASsive hit. We scored 34 rating points, which was the highest for a television episode in the history of Egyptian television. Just to give you a reference, talk shows and comedy shows would average 3 to 4 points. The highest would be 7 to 9 points, for expensive franchises like *The Voice*, *Idol*, and *X Factor*. We averaged 28 to 30 points during the Islamists' reign and continued to shatter those numbers despite the vicious attacks on us. But people who chose denial didn't see that. They were under the impression that the show was no longer watched because their fellow retired friends whom they played golf with had all chosen to boycott the show. For them facts and statistics didn't matter (sound familiar?).

This first episode was all about me trying to find another job—as maybe a football commentator, a fashion designer, a TV chef. In a satirical way I pretended to try other options besides political commentary to avoid talking about Sissi. After all, we just came back from a ban, so I had to play the part of the scared TV host. The joke was simply: Sissi was just everywhere. The videos we got from the networks were talking about Sissi every two minutes. He was on cooking shows, medical shows, at football games, and even had food products named after him. These funny videos gave the audience a taste of what it felt like under that new regime. We showed them that you can't ignore the elephant in the room forever. With Sissi, he was not the elephant in the room, he was the elephant *and* the room.

As I'm sure you could predict, more protests erupted outside my theater. My pictures were burned (again) and banners calling for my death were paraded (again). Interestingly enough, the new laws banning street protests never applied to those people outside my theater. I wonder why?

Bob Simon couldn't believe what he saw, and considering he'd covered every major war zone for the previous forty years, that's saying something. He told me if he didn't know better he would think that someone had created a time machine and shot me back to the McCarthy era. "Hell, even then there were rights," he said. "I would think I woke up in Nazi Germany."

THE PUPPET
THAT ROCKED
THE WORLD

You can exaggerate as much as you want about how a country goes crazy. You can use poetic references from *1984* or real examples from North Korea to show how a country can turn into a zombie state manipulated by media. But nothing can prepare you for what happened in Egypt in the winter of 2014.

By that time the talk shows were all about who wants to destroy Egypt. There were "experts" who would rotate around the different channels and talk about the different kinds of plots being planned against us.

You know those Internet freaks, right? Those who see illuminati signs in Obama scratching his nose with his middle finger? Or those who believe that Madonna climbed thirteen stairs in her VMA awards performance as a sign of Freemasonry? We have the same type of crazy people too, and Madonna is a hot topic for them because after they share the videos of her worshiping Satan they jerk off to the same videos you do. We get it, you are into weird shit.

I understand there are all kinds of crazy Facebook pages that share stupid stories and there are many who believe that kind of shit.

But when that goes mainstream and the media start reporting it as fact, know you are in trouble.

So the story goes like this: After we started our show on YouTube, there was an explosion of talent on the Internet. Everyone seemed to become an Internet celebrity overnight. We had Internet-based comedy shows, singing, music, parody, and our own show hosted many of these talented people as guests.

During the Islamist era we brought on a YouTube sensation called Auntie Fajita. She was a puppet and everybody loved her. Her character was a widow from the Egyptian middle class who had her opinion about everything—love, politics, and even the American elections. The language she used was a play on how some like-minded woman would talk. Think of her as a mixture of the "Church Lady" from *SNL* and Miss Piggy. She was hilarious and extremely popular. She was even starring in commercials for the telecommunications giant Vodafone. The creators of the puppet were friends of mine who worked in an advertising agency.

All of that was working well until the usual dickheads came and spoiled it for everybody.

Auntie Fajita had a Twitter account where she posted her opinions, which were written in the tone of a misinformed middle-class bourgeoise woman.

So, some of those people who have those batshit-crazy Facebook pages started to analyze her tweets and her videos. They postulated that she was speaking in code, that those tweets and her Vodafone commercials were messages to terrorists, who became active in Egypt and started bombing everything.

So far this sounds okay. Every country has its own crazy people. But when the media began using those people's Facebook statuses and quoted them as reliable sources of information, that's when it became disturbing. Many of those crazy people didn't just spring out from nowhere. They were there from the first day of the revolution.

You may recall when I told you that these channels that came out of nowhere were probably funded by the intelligence service? They were always producing these crazy conspiracy theories that "proved" that the whole Arab Spring was an American plan to destroy the Middle East. Many of the owners of those channels and even some of the people who spread those rumors on those channels posed in photos with the highest-ranking generals in the army. You might think that rolling with this story of the puppet was just a media stunt to increase ratings, but when the legal system gets involved, that is when you begin to worry.

The general prosecutor summoned the creators of the Auntie Fajita puppet, and Vodafone found itself in hot water. The prosecutor accused Vodafone of being an accomplice of the puppet, to send hidden messages to the enemies of the nation. It begs the question of who had whose hand up the other's ass?

One of the anchors known to be the mouthpiece of the regime got ahold of the lawyer representing Vodafone and asked him to clarify the position of the company on these allegations. The lawyer laughed. He could not believe that this could be taken seriously. The anchor shouted, "You should not ridicule the Egyptian people. Those are serious charges and we need answers."

This was the state the country was in. A fucking puppet taken in for interrogation. We tried to get the puppet on the show again, but when I invited the creators onto the show, they told me that they couldn't. The lawyer had advised them not to make any public appearances. This shit was real.

Vodafone pulled its TV ad, which was only one ad out of many that were targeted, and it was one company out of many, like Pepsi and Lay's chips and other telecommunications and car companies, who started to have their share of weird accusations. Every slogan was a code; every commercial sound bite became suspicious.

We did the episode anyway, without hosting the puppet. Instead we showed how every commercial was distorted to force people to live in constant fear. To show people the hilarity of targeting those companies, we made a fake commercial ourselves and started to strip away the commentary, the graphics, the music, the sound, until nothing was left. This was the Egypt they wanted: boring and predictable—like a group of brainwashed grandmas eating bowls of oatmeal.

You might think that this "conspiracy" stuff had no effect on regular people. Well, mostly it didn't. Away from television screens people can see through the bullshit.

But there was one thing I saw that triggered us to talk about this nonsense. A military helicopter was gunned down by terrorists in Sinai, about five hours outside Cairo, and four officers were killed. At the funeral and in front of the cameras a wife of one of the officers screamed at the crowd, "They killed my husband, they want to destroy the country. Get them, arrest them, those traitors who help the terrorists. The likes of Auntie Fajita should be brought to justice."

This sounds like what would be a hilarious scene from Trey Parker and Matt Stone's *Team America*, but here no one was laughing.

THE SUPER-
CANDIDATE

Sissi finally decided to run for dictator-in-chief. The people who'd shied away from the word *coup* were now proudly telling us, "Yeah, it's a coup and we like it; it's a dictatorship but we need it." But when people like us, who openly opposed Sissi, called it a military dictatorship, we in turn were called traitors. Many people lost their jobs in the media for merely suggesting what we all knew deep down to be true.

The religious authorities in the Coptic Church and Al-Azhar Mosque were already giving their official seal of holiness on Sissi.

High-ranking Muslim scholars in Al-Azhar made parallels between Sissi and some of the Prophet Muhammad's disciples, and sometimes they elevated him to the same level as prophets.

"When Sissi visited the church, it was like Jesus himself came," the head of the Coptic Church said.

"Sissi is mentioned in the Old Testament, the signs are clear," another priest said.

The Grand Pope of the Coptic Church sent his priests to America when Sissi was visiting the UN to herd the Copts there to rally in solidarity with Sissi, to show America how much he was loved. Most of the Copts who came out had been living in America for decades after filing for political asylum due to religious persecution under the military regime. The same regime they were supporting now. The same military that crushed those twenty-six Christians in front of the TV building only a couple of years ago.

Stockholm syndrome much?

What is wrong with us Egyptians, seriously!

At that time Sissi's pictures were plastered everywhere. On bridges, covering buildings, on cars. It is said that the number and size of a leader's photo are inversely proportional to the freedom of a certain country.

One paper had his photo with the headline: CHRIST THE SAVIOR. Isn't it cool to have a president who, if assassinated, can rise from the grave three days later?

You would think that any self-respecting media figure would criticize the fact that we were turning a blind eye to what was happening. Hell no. As a matter of fact, one of the most popular talk-show hosts admitted that he had no problem whatsoever with the deteriorating state of the country under Sissi. "Yes, I was on Morsi's case when we had power cuts and economic meltdowns. But under Sissi I am willing to ignore this because we support him for a much higher cause. Morsi wanted to sell off the country, he was a traitor. But Sissi is a patriot. We are willing to withstand the harsh economic conditions under him."

Out of nowhere, serious television anchors and talk shows were hosting mystical readers and fortune tellers to talk about the signs laid out by the Zodiac. According to these whack jobs, Sissi was going to be the next president. Considering everything that was happening in the country, you really didn't need any special skills to tell you that he was the president already. Hours and hours of footage were spent on these fame seekers out there to tell us about the "signs." One of them claimed that Sissi was mentioned in an old parchment that was three thousand years old.

The young people who were once at the front line of the revolution were now the black sheep of the pack. The same anchors who earlier had hosted those young people on their shows and glorified the "new young Egypt that was reborn in the hands of these young people" were now openly attacking the youth, asking for the old and senile to rule us because the young just fucked up. A particular journalist who'd been on the front line of the revolution and who pushed for young people to take over was now openly contemptuous of the youth, calling them stupid and in need of proper reform. The same journalist who'd criticized the military for adopting the conspiracy theory talk became one of the regime mouthpieces promoting the idea that the young people were used as tools in those conspiracies.

I couldn't help but recall when the owner of my old channel told me that Egypt didn't need me anymore. Following the media, it seemed that Egypt didn't need its young people either. After all, the "Savior" was here. The regime announced that there would be elections and Sissi announced that he would be running an actual campaign. But it was a campaign that didn't really campaign for anything. He didn't need to. There was no program, no plan, and no fucks given.

"He doesn't need to promise us anything, he is enough"—this was an *actual statement from a talk-show host.*

"How dare you ask the president for a program? He doesn't need us, we need him," another host said.

I was playing these videos on my show and people were laughing. But in the media I was accused of ridiculing Egypt's only hope. Maybe I was harsh? Maybe I shouldn't have associated Sissi with his groupies? Maybe I was wrong? I might have thought so if he himself hadn't gone into an interview saying, "I didn't want to run. The masses asked me to. They pressured me to do it. You can't come now to ask me for any promises. I have none."

The trickery of his language was absurd. Making it sound like he was some hapless man on the street whom the people just happened to propel through the ranks because he was such a martyr for them was insane. He bullied his way into this position of power and now he was acting like someone who forcefully fucked you in the ass and demanded that you be thankful. *And somehow the people were fucking thankful!* I was beside myself with disbelief.

Two years later I was at a Trump rally in a little town in Georgia. The mayor of the town was at the podium warming up the people for the arrival of the Donald. He was shouting and cheering, but he said one thing that brought back those painful memories of Sissi's absurd campaign. He said, "If Donald Trump didn't do anything but build this wall would you still vote for him?" And the people just roared.

With Sissi, he didn't even promise us a fucking wall.

Sure, we still had our interim president, but he was like a ghost. Even for social events that were held under the auspice of the interim president, women came up to recite poetry calling Sissi the future "groom" of Egypt.

These women, who were supposed to be poised and respectful, were dancing outside polling stations chanting Sissi's name and carrying his picture like he was Justin Bieber or some other teenage heartthrob. At the same time they were sticking their tongues out at their own children for "beating" them and proving them wrong. Many of those women turned into hateful, horny fifth-grade bullies.

It was a mystery to me how hate, fear, and absolute infatuation could coexist. Then I read this passage from *1984* that explained why members of the Party were allowed to get married only when the Party had proof that there was absolutely no sexual attraction between the couple involved:

When you make love you're using up energy; and afterwards
you feel happy and don't give a damn about anything. They
can't bear you feel like that. They want you to be bursting
with energy all the time. All that marching up and down
and cheering and waving flags is simply sex gone sour. If you
are happy inside yourself, why should you get excited about
Big Brother and the Three-Year Plans and the Two Minutes
Hate and the rest of their bloody rot?

So, as Orwell said, there is an intimate connection between chastity and political orthodoxy.

Could all those women have miserable sex lives?

If so, it seemed that all of their sexual frustration was being directed toward the biggest love of the country. It didn't matter if what he said in the interviews didn't make sense or some of his solutions were comical. His lovers saw a superhero, whom we were blessed to have. Faith trumps reason. After all, Sissi was the Savior.

Maybe my idea needed to be expanded. We needed male prostitutes wearing Sissi masks to come and secretly pleasure the women into a reason-inducing stupor. Then and only then would the country be ready for a true democracy.

But again, Jesus only walked on water and raised the dead. Our Savior did much more. He cured AIDS!

Don't worry, I'll explain.

WE'VE GOT AIDS!!!

Ultranationalism is a lovely state of mind. It makes you believe that you are the greatest nation on earth. It can drive poor and crushed masses into believing that they are the chosen ones out of billions of people. It can make millions believe that you have defeated the United States of America's Sixth Fleet in the Mediterranean and captured their commander while Obama screamed *uncle* (yes, more of that still to come).

And it can also, magically, cure AIDS.

It was a cold February morning. Writers and producers were in the office discussing the backlash we faced from last week's episode; the fact that we made fun of Sissi's campaign tactics (which could be summarized as "we really don't need a campaign") caused numerous writers and talk shows to unleash their wrath on the show. I mean, how dare we take his pseudo-campaign lightly?

The team settled down and had the usual chat about our previous episode. Now we had a sensitive issue to tackle.

Sissi had just visited Russia. But it was hardly just a visit to share a vodka toast with Putin. The propaganda machine talked about that visit as if we were still in the Cold War. Our TV had 1960s propaganda all over it. If we had black-and-white TV sets we would expect Elvis to pop up. Except now we had an Egyptian Elvis, alive and kicking and wearing black Ray-Bans and posed with Putin for pictures to show Obama that we were moving on.

"Obama is having a nervous breakdown right now," one TV host said.

"According to American newspapers, Obama will shoot himself in the head after Sissi's visit to Russia." That was a headline of a major Egyptian newspaper.

Such was the narrative of our media. According to them, Obama was hoisting a huge boom box outside of Sissi's window blasting Peter Gabriel's captivating, imploring "In Your Eyes."

In America I saw Trump supporters adoring Putin and drawing parallels between him and Trump. I saw it in Egypt way before that.

The narrative of our episode was taking shape. We now knew the kinds of videos we would use. But this time we were really talking about sensitive issues: arms deals, international relations, and refuting the fact that Obama was having a crying fit in the West Wing restroom.

We were once again taking a risk by ridiculing Sissi and his image as conqueror of the world, which was considered by the authorities a national security issue. He was untouchable.

WE WERE STRUGGLING WITH THE SECOND SEGMENT. WE WERE trying to make a mundane education bit work, but there was a lack of decent material and we were really forcing it.

Hend, my producer, rushed into the office. "Bassem, you have to come and see this."

We went out to the hall, where the TV screen was broadcasting a huge press conference. Every single person in that conference was in military attire.

Did we just declare war? No, it was a ceremony to launch a new military hospital.

Another achievement by the army. Interim President Adly Mansour and the de facto president and defense minister, Sissi, were there. It seemed they had just been notified of the discovery of the century and had left the ceremony for the people in charge to announce the amazing news.

An older man in military uniform with a general's rank on his shoulders started to talk. Once he opened his mouth we all had a feeling that he had the air of a hustler or, at best, a con artist who made his way selling junkers at a shady used-car lot. He was introduced as General Dr. Abdel Atti.

He started by stating the fact that Egypt has one of the highest rates of hepatitis C infection in the world. But now we have the cure, he said.

"We have named it CCD. Complete Cure Device."

The pun was quite obvious. *CC* invoked Sissi. How tacky could you get? But oh, it got even better. "This device will cure patients of hepatitis C in a mere few days," Atti said.

Seriously? The most chronic disease known to our country would be cured just like that?

"By June thirtieth there will be no more patients of hepatitis C in Egypt," he announced.

The promised date had *no* relation to the date denoting the anniversary of Morsi being ousted by the army. It was a mere coincidence . . . of course!

"I can also say confidently that this device cures AIDS," Atti continued.

There was a most daunting silence in our hallway as we watched while army generals clapped at that marvelous announcement.

"You see, the AIDS virus is a much weaker virus than hepatitis C virus. If we can cure hepatitis, AIDS is just a piece of cake."

I had to take a seat as I was watching this; it was too much.

"The DNA of hepatitis C is quite similar to HIV," he continued. "That is why our device can work on both viruses. Our device destroys the virus completely in the patient's bloodstream. Now we have free protein DNA floating into the patient's blood. As you know, viruses are made of protein. This free protein nourishes the patient and brings his health back very quickly. It is as if we took the virus away from the patient and returned it to him in the form of a kabab sandwich."

The entire hallway erupted in laughter. Was he trying to be funny or was he trying to give us a heart attack?

"Patients who undergo the treatment are forbidden from eating meat because we are afraid that they will be overloaded with protein. Instead we make them run around the track to burn the extra protein. That is why our patients who get treated with that machine are not emaciated and wasted like other hepatitis and AIDS patients. They are very healthy and gain some muscle mass during the treatment."

Our segment of the week just wrote itself.

I started to assign tasks to the producers and writers and went into my office to recollect my thoughts. Minutes later, Hend came in.

"There is a sort of mutiny in the office," she said with a big smile. "Some of the producers don't want to go with the segment."

I went into the editorial room right in the middle of a heated discussion. "What's wrong, people?" I asked.

"We don't think we should do this segment," my team said.

"But why?" I asked.

Their answers showed me how effective propaganda can be even in the place that is fighting it.

"They are too confident," one producer said. "I know the whole thing sounds stupid. But Bassem, this is . . . the army. They will never announce something like this without being a hundred percent sure."

Many agreed with her.

"What if we made a big deal out of it and then it turned out to be true? We will look really bad then; plus, the army never lies," another producer said.

The army never lies . . . just shows how deep this brainwashing can run.

"I just got off the phone with my parents," a third producer offered. "One of our relatives is infected with hepatitis C. He is very happy with the army invention and can't wait to begin the treatment in a few months. When I told them we are going to talk about it in the show, my parents were furious. They shouted at me, saying, 'Don't you even mention the army in your show. This is the army, they can't be wrong.'"

We were not making fun of desperate Sissi lovers anymore. We were not satirizing the hysteria that made people believe that Sissi was as infallible as a medieval pope. If we did this segment we would be making fun of men in uniform. For Egyptians that was unforgivable.

I brought the discussion to a halt. "Okay guys, I don't want you to think of me as Bassem the TV host. Now I am Bassem the doctor. Let me talk to you about viruses."

For the following thirty minutes, I used a whiteboard to explain what a virus is, what its life cycle is, and why the army's "achievement" was absolute nonsense. They seemed convinced and went back to work. But I knew that this would not be the end of it. My nineteen years of medical education didn't go to waste, see.

The next two days we were pinned in front of our monitors collecting material about the new "invention." It seemed there were actually two devices: a system for diagnosis and a system for treatment. The treatment device was, as I said, appropriately named CCD: Complete Cure Device. This looked like a miserable school project—a makeshift ATM that was executed quite badly.

The "general" who made the announcement earlier posed proudly next to it with other members of the team. He explained how this device worked like a dialysis machine: the blood of the patient passed through the machine, and *voilà!*, it came out free of the viruses.

General Abdel Atti, now identified as the head of the research team, became the star of all the prime-time talk shows. He explained that this machine contained two "elements" with hidden secrets from the days of the pharaohs, which were able to purify the blood of the viruses.

Prominent doctors from university hospitals came to the defense of the new "cure." Hepatologists, cardiologists, and internists who were working under the "general" came out to say how wonderful this invention was. "We have been working on this for twenty-three years," claimed one of them. "We had the results a long time ago but we didn't want to announce it because we feared that it would be stolen from Egypt."

Really? So you had the cure for AIDS right around the time when the whole world was screaming out for relief? Well, thank goodness you kept that shit to yourself—the world needed to see an Oscar-winning performance from Matthew McConaughey in *Dallas Buyers Club*.

The steamed-up general made an appearance at a conference, cameras flashing and microphones peeking out from under his white mustache. He belted out, "I was working in a lab in America. I discovered that invention twenty-three years ago. They offered me two billion dollars to sell the rights to them. I refused and I said my only condition was for this cure to be in the name of an Arab and a Muslim like me. Then the all-mighty Egyptian military intelligence were able to smuggle me outside of the United States. I came here to work for my country, and for the welfare of my people."

This was turning into a very bad sequel of *Mission Impossible*. Who said you needed to be a Scientologist to be that delusional?

The general repeated those claims on another TV show that evening, with the exception that he was offered only $20 million this go-around. I mean, what's a couple of zeros, right?

But that was not all. He also announced a new way to diagnose HIV infection. He claimed to be able to diagnose your condition remotely. Sounds like a *Star Trek* movie, right? Well, wrong. They showed the other miracle device, but it was nothing more than a TV antenna connected to a handle. Yes, a TV antenna that you hold toward the patient. The antenna would just point at and follow you if you had the virus.

This brought to mind a famous scandal in 2008 that involved the all-mighty British Army. A swindler called Jim McCormick sold fake bomb detectors to the British Army in Iraq. He cashed in around 60 million pounds sterling ($80 million U.S.) selling around 6,000 detectors for the price of 10,000 pounds each. The real cost of one device was only around 15 pounds.

Why are all armies stupid? Especially with money?

Now that same fake bomb detector was in the hands of the con artist doctor general in a promotional video made by the army's moral affairs department. He demonstrated how that bomb detector could find out if someone had the virus or not. He pointed it toward one of the patients, telling him, "Congrats, you used to have AIDS, now it is gone."

Apparently, if the antenna didn't point to you, you didn't have HIV.

He then went on to explain how sensitive this detector is. "Even if the patient is in another room, the device will still be able to detect him," he announced proudly. "If there was a trace of the virus on my finger, the device will point at my finger. If I wipe my finger with a tissue, the device will leave my finger and like a hound dog follow the tissue."

Doctors who were trained and educated in prestigious medical schools went out to defend this hoax. They explained how the DNA of each virus had its own electromagnetic wavelength unique to it. The bomb detector could be adjusted for each virus's wavelength and could detect it very accurately.

"Even if the patient was in another room, the detector will point to the patient with the wall separating them," said one doctor, a real fucking doctor, working under that con artist Abdel Atti. This occurred during another prime time talk show. There were two doctors from the team working under General Abdel Atti who went on praising the genius of the general. "You know," one doctor said, "the other day I was in the lab and suddenly I found the machine pointing at me. I was freaking out. But then I remembered that earlier in the day I was greeting General Dr. Abdel Atti, and there must have been some residual virus on his white coat. When he took off the jacket, the antenna pointed to the jacket. This is how accurate our machine is."

We were howling at the videos in the editing room, thinking it could not get any better, when yet another video surfaced. It seems that all of the doctors working on the military team were having a collective orgasm over their fake medical achievement. They couldn't stop calling all of the talk shows to demonstrate how incredible this machine was. "With the same principle of detecting a virus through its electromagnetic waves and hence being able to destroy it, we were able to utilize this principle in curing other diseases," one elated doctor said in a phone call with a TV anchor. "We can also use it to fight bacterial infection."

"Really?" asked the anchor.

"Yes, we have also tried it on many patients with other conditions and they were healed. We have seen patients being healed from lupus, eczema, psoriasis, and diabetes."

"Oh my god," shouted the anchor, "so can it also heal cancer?"

"Of course it can heal cancer," asserted the doctor.

Of course! Why not? Just throw cancer in the mix. Because AIDS, psoriasis, diabetes, and cancer have so much in common and we never knew it. And this has been in the works for the past twenty-three years, but only now are we choosing to reveal it. Aren't we smart?

This turned into a flat-out propaganda hit job by the army, and the military medical team continued to sell the device even more, and it seemed like they never ran out of diseases to cure. "We have noticed that patients with heart conditions and hypertension after being on our treatment for two months stopped their medications because they didn't need them anymore," said the cardiologist on the team.

This was a miracle in the making. A machine that cures viruses, bacterial infections, autoimmune diseases, diabetes, and heart conditions. *You really don't need to sell it harder to us!* But for some reason the military medical team decided to turn this invention into one of those two-for-one infomercial deals with a "But wait—there's more!" special.

"We have also noticed that patients with sexual impotence had major improvement in their sex life," added the same doctor.

That's it, people. This was all we needed. If you say a treatment could also give you a boner, that's all that was needed to sell it, even to healthy people. They might as well have run those interviews as replacements for ExtenZe commercials!

This machine was now named the "Kofta" machine. *Kofta* is another word for "meat" or "kabab," specifically the kind of meat you eat on a skewer in Mediterranean restaurants. This name change happened because of the genius of General Dr. Abdel Atti, who earlier had said that the protein DNA of the virus could, through the treatment, be returned to the patient like a kabab sandwich (or *kofta*).

The Friday of our show people waited to see how we would deal with "Kofta-gate."

We did not disappoint. The audience laughed and howled at every single joke. At the end of the segment I told the audience, "This was all fun and games, but this is so funny that we should actually be serious about it."

I went on to say that this was a scandal, one sponsored by the "most competent institution in the country," an obvious reference to the army. I told the audience that this "cure" was no trial drug. "They said they will cure everyone in June. This is called a promise," I added. "When you make this promise to sick people and you don't deliver, that is a crime in itself, and someone has to be held accountable for that."

The theater was dead silent. The audience clung to every word, as they were thinking, *What? Can we actually hold the army accountable? That's unheard of!*

I went on, "If you think that we will let this go, think again. If you think that we will just be silent until this is forgotten, we won't. Here on this program, we will remind people every single week about this promise until it turns out to be real, or someone is held accountable." The theater exploded with applause.

I was taking this personally because the doctor in me was angry; I hate people being cheated when they are sick. I didn't realize that by speaking out about basic science that we would get even more heat. This was a scandal, and we thought that by doing our job and setting things right we would be praised. But this was the army. The army doesn't give a shit about what is right and what is scientific; they care about their own image even if it's at the expense of the people. Years later I met the scientific advisor of the interim president, who resigned in protest over this scandal. He too had his share of heat. He told me that he met the head of Sissi's office. When he voiced his frustrations about what happened and even brought evidence that this machine doesn't work, he was told: "It doesn't matter if the machine works, what matters is the uniform behind the machine, and this uniform should be respected at all costs."

When I heard this story I was hardly surprised at how all hell had broken loose at the time.

When this episode aired, it set a trend in social media like never before.

"Kofta-gate" was the talk of the town. We realized that if we didn't talk about the machine, it would become another hoax that would be put to sleep. We made it a point to remind people of the "promise" every episode.

The talking heads in the media lashed out against me. They accused me of being a pessimist who was bringing down the morale of the country by laughing at its army.

"If the army says it works, then it works," one anchor would shout on his program.

"You are just jealous of our wonderful army. And to those people I say, die with your viruses," another anchor said with a smirk.

"The cure works," a third anchor would announce, "the security guard at my apartment building has been cured by it."

I didn't know if they were in denial, or if maybe I'd lost my mind and there actually is a new kind of medicine being taught now in medical school and the cure was actually real? I met doctors who were not affiliated with the military medical team, who confirmed that the machine worked.

People had to realize the fallacy of inventing a machine that could cure every known medical malady to man, right?

A shocking fact was revealed over the next few days. The celebrated General Dr. Abdel Atti was not even a doctor. Oh, surprise, surprise. He was a lab technician. He was also a felon accused and convicted of running a sham clinic, where he treated people with herbs without a medical license. His "clinic" was closed down and there was a one-year imprisonment sentence delivered against him.

People wondered how a guy like that could rise in the ranks to make general in the "most efficient and competent establishment" in the country.

But the denial continued.

An anchor proudly announced how Sissi was very happy with the invention, that when he saw it he cried tears of happiness.

It didn't really matter if this was a real invention or not. People just wanted to believe. Months later, when I had to escape the country, a famous TV anchor met me in Dubai and told me that when asked about the AIDS invention in a private meeting with media people, Sissi answered firmly, "The army never announces anything unless we are one hundred percent sure about it."

We kept reminding the audience every week about the approaching June 30 deadline, which was four months away.

The deadline passed but it didn't matter. The army, the media, the overexcited doctors just stopped talking about it. Sissi supporters who were attacking the show for spreading negative energy simply ignored the whole thing. And like that, it was gone.

I felt that what we were doing in the program was amounting to nothing. Yes, people were avidly following us, laughing at every joke and cheering on every bold statement. But what was the use if no one was held accountable for that scandal? This is when I started to lose faith in change. This is when I saw how people were treating the program as simple comic relief, a way to vent, that's all. People who believed us were helpless, and people who loved Sissi no matter what were happy in their own ignorance.

During this whole debacle—I didn't think of North Korea, which I usually did when drawing parallels to our regime. Instead I couldn't help but think of Gambia. Gambia is a small country on the western coast of Africa. In 1994 an army general called Yahya Jammeh took over the country through a military coup, and in 2007 he announced that he had discovered an herbal cure for AIDS. He also announced that hundreds of people were healed. For years this was an undisputed fact in Gambia. WHO workers who objected to that cure were evicted, and those who ridiculed the cure were labeled as part of the "imperial conspiracy" against Gambia. President Jammeh would appear on television with a leather-bound Quran and a long string of beads in front of a group of people with HIV. "In the name of Allah you will be cured in thirty days," he would say, raising the Quran above their heads. The British publication *The Guardian* documented those early days when President Jammeh was rounding up sick Gambians to cure them: "Waiting outside Mr. Jammeh's treatment chamber, the patients themselves said they did not need laboratory results to tell them they felt better. 'It feels as if the president took the pain out of my body,' a patient would say."

Many poor Egyptians stopped taking their hepatitis C treatment. "Why spend the money? The army will heal us for free," they collectively believed.

Reports of hundreds of Egyptians with deteriorating health conditions came to light after the army failed to deliver on its promise. They dared not submit complaints against the army.

The television anchors that sold the idea of the cure are still around today, screaming and kicking and finding another bullshit conspiracy to distract the people with. No one was ever held accountable and, as usual, the army and Sissi were untouchable.

Every time I read about another hepatitis C patient who was in a deteriorating condition because he waited for the army cure which never came, I go back to *The Guardian* report about Gambia and the promise of the thirty-day cure. The last few lines in the report went as follows: "Amadou Jallow, 25, who quit his job at a tourist hotel after his mother was diagnosed with AIDS. In his savings account is 8,000 dalasis (about £150)—enough, he says, to last him the 30 days Mr. Jammeh promises it will take to heal his mother. 'I'm just afraid that, what if my account runs low?' he says. 'But by then I think she will be cured.'"

I-LISTEN

Okay—we are all pretty familiar with the NSA now that Joseph Gordon Levitt played Snowden in an Oliver Stone film. So, remember when Obama was apparently listening in on your phone calls and even tapping into the calls of world leaders? The NSA listening in on the American public was a topic everybody was talking about in Egypt. Not because it was happening in the States, but because it was used to justify what was happening there.

For over a year after June 30, 2013, when the coup occurred, some of the worst people were on the front lines of the media scene. They were usually deadbeat journalists whom everyone knew were associated with our own NSA and even our intelligence service. Suddenly those people were given airtime and their programs were heavily financed. One of those third-grade journalists was hosting a show called *The Black Box*. This show did one thing and one thing only: it broadcast private phone calls of public figures, specifically those who were vocal against the regime. Now, let's get one thing straight here. No one can record all those calls from different people unless that person is someone at the highest levels of power. Our own NSA was famous for recording private phone calls and using them to pressure media figures, political leaders, people in the op-position, and basically anyone who would not play along. But now corruption had reached a new level of scum. Those private phone calls were broadcast on a prime-time TV show to entertain people while they ate their dinner.

The government allowed it, and "patriotic" citizens supported it and even rooted for it to continue. A spokesman of the police said, "If you are not doing anything wrong you shouldn't worry if your calls are recorded or not."

The neo-fascists who revolted a year earlier against a religious rule that might take away our freedoms and violate our personal lives were welcoming the recording and broadcasting of people's private lives. "We need to know who are conspiring against our nation," Sissi supporters would tell you. "If they were innocent they would have nothing to hide." That was the new standard of "human rights" in this country. Don't do, say, or think anything bad and we won't fuck you up.

People went to court to stop *The Black Box*, but the court, and the law, belonged to the state. "This is a form of investigative journalism," the court ruled.

We were the only program that came out and derided that show. We showed our audience what a world of free-for-all information would be like, not to mention what a douchebag this two-bit journalist and the others who supported him were. Then, at the end of our program, we displayed the most common arguments those assholes use. A pro-Sissi TV anchorwoman said, "It happens everywhere else. America is doing it, the NSA is doing it. Here are your 'democratic countries' listening in to their citizens, so we are justified in doing it."

Yes, but they don't broadcast it in prime time, you dim-fucks!

PULLING THE PLUG

As if it were a surprise. There were signs, very strong signs . . .

Working on the show was becoming increasingly difficult. The more popular it got, the more hated it became. It continued to break viewership ratings and it had the most expensive price for television advertisement in Egyptian television history. Anyone would have been elated to have this show. But with me it was different.

I always had haters and people who'd prefer to see me dead in a gutter. I get that, but to be so childish as to jam our satellite signal? The opening credits would play and suddenly the signal would be lost. This had never happened on TV before.

We filed a complaint to the Egyptian media authority, which said they would investigate the incident. Of course they never got back to us.

The pro-military shows started to host "experts" who hinted that all the dissidents would "disappear" soon, including my show.

"The people don't want him anymore," they would say. By the "people" they meant the regime.

So far we had been following a conservative strategy. We couldn't ridicule Sissi directly since he was not president yet. We were careful not to even get him onscreen and make fun of what he was saying while he was in his military uniform. He needed to be out of uniform, and above all he needed to be sworn in for the gloves to come off.

We were approaching our first break in weeks, a scheduled and much-needed two-week holiday around Easter, away from a very stressful job. As the break swiftly approached, we had a team meeting to decide what to do next.

Then we got a call. The network asked us to "delay" our return. It seems that they were under a lot of pressure from the authorities. "We need to show goodwill," they told me. "We want you to come back after the elections are over. We would announce that we did that because we didn't want to influence the outcome."

Of course that was bullshit. Everyone knew the outcome of the elections. There was no way anyone could affect them. Sissi was running "virtually" unopposed. And by *unopposed* I meant that he was running against a ghost of a candidate. One of the candidates in the previous elections had agreed to run against him, perhaps to give some legitimacy to the whole process. Remember, appearances are all that matter (Jesus—it sounds like we are a heartless pageant mom). If Sissi ran alone it wouldn't look good in front of the global community. Still, the outcome was a joke: Sissi won by 98 percent of the vote. The "challenger" came in third. Yup, in a two-man race the other candidate came in third when the ballots were counted. There were more disqualified ballots than the ones he got. It was a fucking joke.

So now we were back and we wrote an incredible episode. I can say that because you will never see it. Actually, no one will. But in my opinion it was one of the most daring and funniest ones we ever wrote. We were breaking so many taboos that I was sure I would end up in jail for it. This time we didn't hold back. We got Sissi right there with all the pageantry and empty promises. We were in satire heaven.

Then another phone call came. "Bassem, we are sorry, we have to shut you down."

A FAREWELL
TO ARMS

I couldn't decide how that phone call made me feel. Was it a sense of deep sadness because they were taking away the thing I loved doing, the thing that I succeeded in, and the legacy that I created? Or was I relieved from the horrible stress I was under all the time?

I couldn't really decide. I still can't.

The show was gone. I was told that the owner of the network received the call from an army general who was running Sissi's office. He asked if I was coming back to mock Sissi, and the owner told him he didn't know but it would be very hard to avoid the topic. The general told the network owner that they "don't prefer" my return. When the owner told him that if the network shut us down, other channels would jump on the opportunity to sign up the most watched show on television. His answer was, "Well, believe me, no other channel will dare to do that."

Funny, Americans ended up with a president who bitches and whines about unflattering pictures, mean jokes, and *SNL* sketches where he's played by Alec Baldwin; whereas in Egypt it takes a phone call from the president's secretary to shut down political satire in the whole country.

Dictators are so thin skinned, aren't they?

Now, I could be lying. As a matter of fact, I am making all that up. I am victimizing myself and covering for my failures because I am an attention whore. This is what the Sissi-blind lovers would tell you: "Do you have proof for what you are saying?" Well, I am not in the habit of recording and broadcasting phone calls and private meetings like their beloved authority would do . . . so no. Even if I had gone public with this information at the time, the network would say that I was lying because they would have faced a lot of trouble exposing this story.

The denial machine was ready: "He was shut down because no one was watching him anymore."

"It is a Saudi channel; Egypt had no control over it."

"He was paid five million dollars to shut up. He has no principles."

Well, Allah knows I wouldn't be writing this book for the shitty advance HarperCollins gave me if that were the case!

I was not the only one shut down. I was the last of a long chain of TV hosts who were knocked off the air because they didn't follow the crowd. But there was always a justification for each one: bad ratings, a false sense of victimization, financial problems with their respective networks. You name it.

We held a press conference to announce the end of the show. Out of respect for our network we agreed that we wouldn't talk about what happened between us behind closed doors. It would just get them into too much trouble.

I went out into that press conference saying that ending the show was a defeat. But it wasn't a defeat for us, it was a defeat for a regime that was supposed to be more powerful than us. I said that ending the show was a louder message than anything that could have been said. "Message delivered," I declared.

We had invited everyone from local and international media. The international media put the story in their headlines while it was ignored locally. One of my researchers who worked closely with a state-run newspaper told me that there were clear orders to ignore that press conference. If it wasn't reported, it didn't happen.

As I took the stage for the last time to speak to the reporters I tried to retain my composure (and smile!). I was quick with my jokes and even threw a couple of indirect punches at Sissi, which everyone applauded. I asked my crew to come onstage for a final photo together.

After the reporters left I spent over two hours comforting my team. They couldn't believe the show was over. I tried to joke around with them. We took group photos and selfies. We hugged, giggled, and joked around to make it easier.

Then everyone left. I was alone in the theater. The security guards told me my car was outside, waiting to take me home. I asked for a couple of minutes. "I need to get something from my dressing room," I told them. I went backstage for the last time and looked around at those walls that would soon no longer host the show. I went into my dressing room and switched off the lights. And for the next ten minutes I let myself go, and cried.

A TOXIC BRAND

Initially, unemployment doesn't feel that bad. There are no deadlines and no real commitments. I welcomed the stress-free life at first but soon found out that it wasn't a viable option for somebody who needed to make fun of things.

Only a few days after I stopped doing the show offers came pouring in from Arabic-speaking channels based in Europe and the United States. There were even serious offers from Muslim Brotherhood–funded channels that were now broadcasting from Turkey to bring back the show on their screens for any figure I asked. These were the same Brotherhood channels that had cursed me day and night and accused me of having blood on my hands. They accused anyone who had criticized Morsi of being an accomplice to the coup and had selective amnesia in terms of their army ass-licking days.

I couldn't take this show outside of Egypt. Despite all the craziness that was happening there, I would've been looked at as a dissenting fugitive had I gone elsewhere. It didn't matter how stupid and ridiculous those accusations were. Egypt had proven time and time again that this madness eventually takes its toll on people. For a regime like Sissi's, it was in their best interest to prop up imaginary enemies all the time to keep people distracted. A satirist fleeing from the country and getting funding from abroad to attack them would be the perfect gift.

Those were not speculations. The regime actually issued laws that could basically put *anyone* in jail. One of those laws was targeted at anyone who received funding from abroad to get involved in activities that might result in tarnishing the image of the country through spreading false news, incitement of hate, disturbance of the peace, or *anything else.* "Anything else" was an actual phrase in the law.

You could be sentenced to life in prison or even executed if it was "proven" that those activities qualified as an act of treason. I could be invited to dinner by a foreign human rights group and that could qualify as my receiving foreign funding, or I could make a joke that could be considered an "embarrassment" to the regime.

I decided I would not do the show outside the country. After all, was it worth it? I'd had the most popular show in the Arab world. Had it made a difference to the cause? Did it protect me when I was censored? Did it stop the madness? I was just sick and tired of sticking my neck out for no reason. I was a satirist, not a freedom fighter. I know this might not sound very inspiring, but when your own parents still buy into the propaganda no matter what you do, and even some of your extended family members share posts on Facebook accusing you of treason, well, that can make you question a lot of things.

My fears were confirmed only a few weeks later. I was invited to give the keynote speech at two important conferences in Europe: the Global Media Forum in Bonn and the Oslo Freedom Forum in Norway. I decided that I should have a conservative strategy when I spoke abroad. In no way was I in the mood to confront the regime.

In Germany I avoided mentioning any specific names and speaking openly about what had happened to me or what was happening in Egypt. I told my interviewers beforehand to avoid asking any confrontational questions and that I would give them what they wanted by speaking indirectly about my situation. It worked. The interviews and the speeches were well executed, and anyone with half a brain would understand exactly what I was talking about.

Back in Egypt, people with half a brain were pissed enough to make a move. The production company that used to produce the show was raided the next day after my appearance in Germany. The raid occurred under the pretense of someone "using a non-original version of Microsoft Windows software." A couple of people were arrested and the computers and other equipment confiscated. It should be a crime to use Microsoft Windows in today's day and age, but not enough to arrest innocent employees!

Amr, my executive producer, was summoned to the police station. The officer there openly told him that they did what they did because of me. "Let Germany get you out of that trouble," the officer said. "It's a warning this time, but if Bassem doesn't shut up, we will be more severe next time."

Amr begged me to let it go. "Every time you speak, it hurts us," he said.

I was blackmailed through my friends and family in Egypt. Maybe it was too much trouble to arrest me, but it was easy for the authorities to pressure me through my loved ones. They'd done this before when they arrested Tarek's family members in order to get to me, so why wouldn't they do it again?

A month later, I went on my scheduled trip to Oslo. I didn't once mention the word *Egypt* and I actually gave a good speech that served my message without saying anything specific.

Apparently, I was mistaken. On the way back to Cairo I didn't realize that this would be the last time I would see my country.

TO FLEE OR
NOT TO FLEE

All the time while I was doing my show on a different channel and fighting all those fuckers that sucked up to the regime and facing public rage, I had forgotten that I was in the middle of a legal battle.

When the first channel, CBC, banned my show a year earlier, we went to court to settle that dispute through an arbitration case. Meanwhile, I went to host my final season on MBC until I was banned again, but this time under friendlier conditions, in which the network and the show had mutually consented to end things peacefully. All that time the arbitration case with CBC was going on. This was a commercial arbitration case, so basically it was a game of numbers and figures to decide who breached the contract and who hurt the other party financially. With my limited understanding of the law that was what I thought.

Well, I thought wrong.

The final verdict was overdue. Since I had started traveling to Europe and the States to do speaking engagements, the verdict had been delayed and rescheduled more than three times. After my speech in Oslo I was invited to speak in the United States for a number of events. My return to Egypt was to be on the tenth of November. The verdict was delayed further, to be announced on the eleventh. I landed in Cairo on the tenth around midnight and slept. The next day I woke to Tarek's phone call (he was still a fugitive in Dubai) asking me to be on a conference Skype call in our company's headquarters in Cairo in an hour. "Bassem, it is important, we need you there. I can't speak on the phone."

So I went to the company with absolutely no clue what was going on.

I walked into a room full of long faces: the members of the board, the CFO, the media representative, the operational manager, and Tarek on the other side of the call.

"Bassem, we lost the arbitration," they told me as I went in. "They slammed us with a one-hundred-million-pound fine and you are obligated to pay half." The verdict was so skewed that it held me accountable to pay the whole lot if the company defaulted.

"How could we lose?" I asked.

"Bassem, it was out of our hands. This verdict was manipulated. It was totally politicized," the lawyer told me.

They handed me a page of the verdict that discussed the importance of "national pride" and "how the country should get together to face the imminent dangers," and how "satirical shows are only fit for advanced countries but in countries like ours such shows are counterproductive and may cause public unrest and disrupt the peace."

This was no legal verdict. This was no arbitration decision. This was a page of cheap propaganda. Not only was the verdict unprofessional, but it was an insult to Egyptians in suggesting that we are not mature enough to take a joke.

"Bassem, you need to leave the country right now," Sherif, our CFO, told me. "We have taken the liberty to book you a flight to Dubai to be with Tarek. I don't think it is safe for you here."

"But could they arrest me?" I asked.

"Listen," the lawyer told me, "under the law and under normal conditions they cannot arrest you or put you on a no-fly list. They can confiscate your assets and that's it. However, with all the craziness happening here they can arrest you or at least prevent you from traveling under a heavy cover of propaganda. No one will ask complex legal questions. For the masses you are now a convict and the 'law should be respected.'"

"Your flight is in four hours. I suggest you pack," Sherif said abruptly.

For the next four hours I was in a state of shock. I can't even remember what I did and how I did it. I stopped by my dad's to tell him I was fleeing the country. He also was in shock, but I only had a few minutes for a final good-bye. There was no time to see my brother, so I told Dad to fill him in. Just like that, the time with my father was over.

I went back home and asked my wife to help me pack whatever I could get into two suitcases. I had to explain to her what was happening while I frantically threw stuff in my suitcases. It was a terrible feeling. Why should I be the one escaping in the middle of the night like a drug dealer or a corrupt politician? All I did was make jokes.

My wife was unusually calm. She was just too cool for all of what was happening. When I asked her about this she said, "Well, at least you are not being arrested or shot. Many of the people we know now are in prison or even shot in the middle of a demonstration. Traveling is temporary, I can deal with that."

Sometimes you remember all the awesome reasons that made you fall in love with your wife. That was one of those moments.

"Are you sure you didn't forget anything?" she asked me as I was rushing out the door.

"With that frantic packing? I am dead sure I forgot a lot," I answered jokingly.

Thank god my three-year-old daughter was too young to understand all of this.

Abbas, my old friend, came with me to the airport. He wanted to be there to ask for assistance in case I was arrested.

Was my name already on the list? Would they let me fly? I didn't know what to expect. The verdict had come out only a few hours earlier.

Remember how I started this story, this book? Me in a car wondering if I would be able to get on that plane? Well, by the grace of some benevolent being, I got on it.

I headed to Dubai. When I landed there, social media was already buzzing about the verdict. The usual propaganda websites and state-run networks were describing me as a fugitive who had escaped a legal verdict. A regular comic on the run.

WATCHING THE CRAZINESS FROM A DISTANCE

In the two years since I left Egypt, things haven't gotten better. Thousands of people have been incarcerated for the most trivial reasons. Hundreds have been tortured on a daily basis in police stations. Others have been killed.

You would think that there would be some sort of stability on the surface at least. You know, the kind of fake stability military dictatorships have. But even economically the army was running the country into the ground. They were basically milking the shit out of it, changing laws, basking in the corruption that is protected by their military status. Every day, people woke up to a new business taken by the army.

The regime was telling us that no matter what happens, we are still better than Syria and Iraq. They were the new boogeymen now.

But we were actually turning into Syria or Iraq, without any outside military interference or an inside civil war. The military supporters still lack any thoughts resembling logic. They are part of the same echo chamber you'd find yourself in if you attended a Trump rally: "Everyone is conspiring against us. They are out to get us, they hate us for our freedoms." Even when Sissi visited Germany and the media there grilled him for all the human rights violations, Egyptian media accused the German media of being funded by Islamists!

Fascism was coveted and promoted like never before. In the same way that white supremacy and racism and bullying were normalized for Trump supporters. Many media figures accompanied the president to China. They came back marveling at how strong China is. "China was doing just fine with no democracy," they said. "They even shut down social media and Facebook and YouTube. They don't need it there. We should do the same."

In Egypt, North Korea was not a joke; it was an example to follow. In one incident an Egyptian judge sentenced more than five hundred people to death in less than twenty minutes. They were all accused of killing one police officer. *One!*

Young people were taken from their houses in the middle of the night and disappeared for months. They then appeared in a propaganda video produced by the military, in which they "confessed" to taking part in terrorist plots, and pictures were taken of them with a variety of weapons, as though they were being photographed for a spread in a monthly publication of "Terrorism Today." They were later filmed "confessing" to their evil deeds. Many of their families came out and said that those confessions were tortured out of them.

You didn't even have to participate in a political activity to be taken into custody. A twenty-two-year-old college student was arrested for photoshopping Mickey Mouse ears onto Sissi's head. They looked really good on him. Still, that kid was sentenced to three years in jail.

Army generals appeared on television to claim there is a "Supreme Council of the World" that controls everything, that decides which country they want to bring down.

Sissi warned Egyptians that we are facing a "Fourth Generation war"—whatever the hell that means—and hinted that those who opposed his rule were spies or were affiliated with the Muslim Brotherhood.

The media were creating a new breed of citizens. We were now a nation of informants.

Border control officers in the Cairo airport bragged about their "catch of the day" on the pages of newspapers. That "catch" could be little remote-control helicopters and drone toys, you know, those toys being sold at Brookstone? The photos appeared under a headline saying BORDER CONTROL EXPOSES A DEVIOUS PLOT TO SMUGGLE SPY DRONES INTO THE COUNTRY.

The paranoia spread like wildfire among regular Egyptians. All they heard on television was that there was a global conspiracy against Egypt, so it is only natural that they would go out into the streets seeking to save their country.

English once again became a dangerous language to speak in public. A British couple was captured and delivered to the police by "concerned citizens" in the subway who'd overheard the two talking in their own language, you know, English.

You see, America, you are not the only country to throw people off planes for speaking another language.

I still had a share of accusations directed at me too. Although I was thousands of miles away from Egypt, the media hit men were all over my case. They would refer to me as the "American poster child." One TV host said, "America always takes care of its men in Egypt, and Bassem Youssef is living proof of that."

Madness is now everywhere. It is the kind that makes people believe anything out of fear and hysteria. Like that time the army told the Egyptian people that they had defeated the American Sixth Fleet . . .

That's right. We defeated your troops in a war you *never knew anything about*. One of the famous pro-military TV hosts appeared on his show holding a copy of Hillary Clinton's memoir *Hard Choices*. He announced that according to this book America tried to send the Sixth Fleet to invade Egypt and reinstate Morsi. However, the Egyptian army under Sissi prevented this invasion and even managed to capture the commander of the Sixth Fleet through a special operation. We threatened that we would expose America's defeat to the world if they didn't retreat, which they did. And that would have been so, so, so cool. If only it had happened.

The TV anchor actually had an easy time getting away with this by citing Clinton's book, because not a single person has read that book. Have you read that book? I haven't. Literally, no one.

Everyone was living in a parallel reality. But something had to give. Everything in the country was falling apart. The economy was going down the drain; prices were rising by the minute. Many were starting to see this regime for what it really is, a failure. But the military wouldn't accept that. In their book and the book of their staunch supporters the country was fine.

When they ran out of tricks and people started to really feel the hardship with the worsening economy, the police announced they had arrested twelve people who they accused of plotting to spread a "pessimistic mood" in the country. According to the government there were no shortages of goods, no devaluation of currency, and no collapse in services and infrastructure; it was all an illusion propagated by twelve traitors. As usual they had people on camera confessing (probably out of fear of torture) that they had plotted to spread rumors daily to destroy the "morale of the public."

You might ask yourself, how come the supporters of such a regime don't see all of this? Well, the military always had an explanation for everything, even for the most absurd things. They would believe the military no matter what happened. Even if the military's lies were exposed. I will give you an example.

In the fall of 2015 the military proudly announced that they had a successful airstrike, killing a terrorist cell in the Egyptian Western Desert. This was a common occurrence. Some people would be killed somewhere and the military or the police would simply say they were terrorists. There was no other source than the military, and no one dared to question that. After all, the people killed in these raids or attacks are Egyptians who are worth nothing to the regime. Everything was justified by "national security." But this time, those who were killed in the airstrike turned out to be Mexican tourists who were on an off-road trip. Since there was a foreign government involved they couldn't say that those people were just some terrorists.

The Mexican foreign minister flew to Egypt to deliver a very harsh message to Sissi for this fuckup. What happened then was absolutely ridiculous. As Sissi was photographed with the Mexican minister, with his face showing that he was shitting in his pants, the Egyptian media pushed the narrative that Mexicans are known to be drug dealers and those who were killed must have been there illegally. Even after the military's initial lie about the victims being terrorists was exposed, the military supporters just believed the new narrative that *we killed a bunch of drug dealers*. Hmm, Mexicans being drug lords? Supporters who would believe anything? Why is this so familiar?

Oh yes . . . The Trump wagon!

When I came to America, I witnessed all of Trump's scandals, including the famous tape in which he was bragging about grabbing women by the pussy. I saw a Trump supporter listening to the tape and saying that she still supported Trump. He had been chosen by Jesus to save America. No matter what Trump (or Sissi) does, their supporters will never change their positon.

Stupidity is not exclusive to the Middle East.

I was watching all of this and thanking God I didn't have my show. I would have had endless material, but every joke I would've had to make would've brought me closer to jail.

And yet, they asked me to come back. The intelligence service contacted me this go-round. What a shocker.

MY OWN LITTLE CURSE

It was early 2015, three months after I escaped the country, and I was watching the lunacy that is the Egyptian media and regime from Dubai. I was still there trying to make ends meet. Dubai isn't the cheapest city in the world, and I was slammed with legal fees fighting that stupid verdict to prevent the authorities from confiscating my belongings in Egypt.

The funny thing was that I was struggling financially while huge contracts were thrown my way. I was offered the slot as host for "*SNL* Arabia" in the Middle East, under one condition: no political satire. I was living a paradox of struggling financially while refusing multimillion-dollar deals for light comedy shows and offers for game shows. Hell, I was even asked to be a judge on the Arab *X Factor*.

Albernameg was my blessing and my curse. I knew that if I were onscreen people would expect me to talk about the political madness and not politely joke about some trivial celebrity gossip or fluff piece. Many accused me of selling out and not continuing with the show abroad. I had seen people follow the fervor pushing them to do more, who ended up in jail, and all they got was a hashtag for their name. People will dare you to fight their battles but in the end you will find yourself alone.

I received yet more devastating news: my dad was hit by a car in Cairo. He died immediately.

After years of dealing with death within this revolution I was numb. I actually saw my dad's death as a blessing, a way to take a rest from this maddening world, a break from the Zombie Land Egypt has become. My dad belonged to that older generation that yearned for "stability." A military dictatorship for them is better than the uncertainty and the chaos that a revolution brings.

My dad and I had our arguments but they were far less heated than the ones I had with my mom. They were always solved by a couple of free tickets for the show! In less than eighteen months I lost both of my parents. This might have been a sign. Maybe it was better to break whatever ties I still had with the place I used to call home. Maybe it was my parents bidding me farewell and asking me to look forward instead of looking back at the past. My parents left this life healthy, strong, and independent. How many people can say that? They were the best parents. They carried my burden all their lives and when they left, they left easily and swiftly and without burdening others.

I wanted to go back and bury my father but I was afraid of being arrested upon arrival. My brother urged me not to come back. I had to comply but couldn't help but feel guilty. Only a few months earlier a friend of mine, an activist, was arrested on arrival because he had come back to visit his sick mom. Egypt for me had turned into Hotel California: you could check in anytime you like, but you can never leave!

WE ARE SORRY, WE WANT YOU BACK

Over the nine-month period since I'd left Egypt, I was approached three times by the Egyptian intelligence service urging me to come back. I would get a call or a request to meet people connected to the intelligence service, telling me that they were "authorized" to find out if there was a possibility for me to come back to Egypt.

This has been a strategy all too familiar in Egypt. Get ahold of the dissidents and give them a spot to show the world that the regime is democratic. But bit by bit this dissident will be tamed and eventually controlled. Here we are back to the dog analogy.

When I was fighting with my previous channel a famous anchor with the channel called me and asked me to take it easy. "We all know that you are right to speak up," he told me, "but sometimes when the wind is too strong, you need to bend down. We need to stay in the game, to push forward other issues. We can't solve everything at once."

This guy had been on the airwaves for more than fifteen years. He represented everything I hated about media in the Arab world.

"Well, with all due respect," I answered, "when you bend down once, you stay bent, you never stand tall again. You have been around for too long not to know that."

I wonder why he stopped calling . . .

Time after time, the intelligence service sent their people to talk to me. By then the huge popularity of Sissi was slipping. The economy was going to the crapper and even the rich, well-to-do people were getting fed up with everything. Their media tools were losing their credibility fast and the regime needed a face-lift.

"They realize that the way they dealt with you was wrong, they are willing to give you whatever guarantees you need," the mediators told me.

I asked them if I would have absolute freedom with my content and they answered that there should be some sort of "understanding" and that we all needed to work for the "good of the country." The "understanding" would basically mean that I would be appointed some officer looking over my scripts, and the "good of the country" would be a thick black marker. I didn't trust them. I knew they would use me to whitewash their tyrannical acts.

The last time they approached me, I had had enough. I told the caller that if the regime didn't intend to release the people in jail and ask other journalists and activists who fled the country to come back, in addition to starting a real investigation into their human rights violations, they should just go fuck themselves. I didn't hold back with the Sissi bashing either. The guy on the phone was appalled at the number of F-words I threw his way.

I knew my calls were monitored but I didn't care; I wanted them to hear it. I knew they wanted me on-air again, under their control, totally castrated. They wanted to show the world that "hey, your Egyptian Jon Stewart is back." I was their decoy.

I couldn't do that. Not because I was a freedom fighter or, god forbid, I had a conscience or even principles. No, I refused because when a satirist is not allowed to speak freely about what matters to the people, he ceases to be a satirist; he becomes a mere distraction. Many comedy shows launched after my show ended. All were simple, "safe" social comedies, where they totally ignored the disaster that is Sissi and just focused on making fun of the citizens. I couldn't do that. I would have lost whatever self-respect I still had.

Since I didn't have a regular show at the time, I put together a one-man show. It was a mix of a standup, storytelling, and a think piece to reflect on the madness of the media during the Arab Spring. I would satirize the media during the Mubarak, the Muslim Brotherhood, and the Sissi eras. The shows were all a great success but there was one problem. The intelligence service sent people to heckle me and try to spoil the show. This was a page right out of the book of the former Soviet Union propaganda machine. Intelligence used the same people to hold rallies for Sissi whenever he visited Western capitals.

I was warned of this before I got onstage. The hecklers' aim was to get a thirty-second bite on camera; one would call me names or shout at me and try to get a reaction, while another would covertly shoot the whole thing on his phone.

Knowing this beforehand I maintained my composure and I even made fun of them, turning them into the laughingstock of the theater, but it didn't matter. The video made it to the state-run media, and I looked as if I was about to be kicked out by the audience.

Headlines like EGYPTIANS REJECT BASSEM YOUSSEF JOKES AGAINST SISSI or BASSEM YOUSSEF EVICTED FROM A SHOW BECAUSE OF ANGRY AUDIENCE made it into Egyptian newspapers. As per usual, the truth didn't really matter. It was all for the propaganda.

I couldn't believe that a regime with all of its resources had turned into sulking middle-school cry babies who just wanted to get back at people they didn't like.

I didn't feel safe in the Middle East anymore. I decided to take my "toxic" brand elsewhere. I saw that a certain country was experiencing its own version of hate, xenophobia, and fascism. Maybe not as widespread as in Egypt, but they were getting there. So I packed my bags and decided to move to America!

AMERICA: A DIFFERENT KIND OF CRAZY

I received an offer from Fusion Television, a part of a bigger network that includes Univision and the *Onion*. I asked them if they were serious or if it was a stunt for the *Onion* fake news! They were more than serious. They wanted me to host a show that satirizes American politics from a Middle Eastern perspective. The show would be called *Democracy Handbook*.

I got to travel around America, attend Trump rallies, the Republican and the Democratic national conventions, and the like. It was such a fun experience to see the American democracy at work. But as I was inside the Republican convention it was déjà vu for me—listening to Trump, Gingrich, Giuliani, and the rest of the who's who of "who the hell are those people" taking the stage one after the other gave me the jitters. I would sometimes translate parts of their speeches in my head and they would sound exactly the same as the ones I heard back home. The fear, the xenophobia, the hate, they all came in different shapes and forms; only, they were wearing more expensive suits and had much pastier skin.

When I heard that many Americans, like many Egyptians, believe that Obama is a secret Muslim Brotherhood member, I never thought I would actually meet those people in real life. I interviewed people at Trump rallies who believe that there are at least thirty-five to forty ISIS training camps inside the United States, all sanctioned by the black Muslim president.

The stupidity was not limited to some "fringe" supporters. On Fox News I found an abundance of stupidity and ignorance. I discovered the simplistic way Americans look at the Middle East. And I get asked a lot if it is better to have a military or an Islamic government in Egypt, but people don't realize that it is just one and the same. Many think that it is better to have a military dictator in the Middle East to protect against fundamentalists. The thing is, military regimes in the Middle East *are* fundamentalists. The way they used the religious groups and the Salafi sheikhs to keep people under control is in and of itself one of their strongest weapons. The way they use Al-Azhar Mosque (our own version of the Vatican) and the Coptic Church to curb people's right to speak freely is no different from what the Muslim Brotherhood wanted to do. One used the gun to get to power then protects it with religion, and one used religion to get to power then protects it with the gun.

Under religious regimes, when things go really badly, people start to ask why God isn't helping them now that they are pious and religious. (I mean, isn't Islam the solution for everything?) When that happens, the religious authorities tell the people that it's their own fault, that they are not religious enough and that this is a "test from God that we need to overcome."

It's the same under military rule. When Sissi's regime destroyed the Egyptian economy and when people started to scrape for food, TV anchors, with their fat paychecks, told people that it was their own fault, because they were asking for too much: "It's not the time to ask for three whole meals now," one anchor said. "The country is in a critical situation and you should consider the worsening economic conditions as a test from God. Don't you have enough faith?" The tricks are the same, the bullshit is the same.

Many Americans ask me, "What can we do in the Middle East? How can we help?"

This is not an easy question to answer. And remember, this is not a book with real solutions. I am a satirist, at the end of the day, and I am not capable of giving you a fancy solution loaded with political jargon.

But I can tell you that whatever America is doing, it's not working. The West is in love with this idea of dealing with "one entity" that can guarantee stability—whether this entity is a military regime, a strong Islamic political group, or a monarchy that uses religion to control its people. America supports those regimes for the fake promise of stability and to guarantee its own interests. But this stability comes with a price. For these regimes stability means the elimination of any form of free speech. The Middle East has been a dangerous place to ask any questions about religion or the military for the past sixty years. If you ask questions you are either a traitor, an infidel, or both. It's like that Salafi who couldn't handle my questioning on how Sharia is not compatible with modern life, or the pro-military people who couldn't imagine that the army could lie to them about that AIDS cure.

Fact-checking the authorities is looked upon as a form of mutiny against the country or against God. They will always find a way to justify ridiculous claims. If you challenge those claims, you don't like the country or you are misinformed by "mainstream media," which is not telling you the "truth." When I see Trump making things up, like claiming that Obama created ISIS, and people believe him and even claim that the media are covering it up, it is no different from what I saw at home. Whenever his supporters were faced with facts and reality they would simply tell you that this is the talk of liberal media who hate Trump and who hate America. Same as with military supporters in Egypt, whenever you give them a glimpse of how the real world outside views our regime as a pathetic joke they immediately tell you that it's just part of a global conspiracy against Egypt.

This is a result of continuous infusion of hate, but before you hate you first need to fear. And this is what all these regimes in the Middle East, or even Trump in America or those pro-Brexit politicians in Britain are so good at. Fear has always been their best weapon. Fear of refugees, of people who don't look like us, fear of "losing our religion and identity," fear of war, and the destruction that will happen if you don't blindly follow your dictator, or simply the fear arising from dealing with facts, reality, and science, because truth is not really their friend.

Satire is a great antidote to that fear mentality. When you laugh, you are not afraid anymore. Dictators are afraid of jokers. Laughing in the face of tyranny and fear disarms them in front of their supporters. Ridiculing them, making fun of them, and questioning their empty rhetoric exposes them and sends them running naked through the streets. They come back at you with all their might because it is much more than their image or dignity that they want to preserve: their legitimacy is at stake. That's why they try to belittle you, bring you down, and destroy your image in front of their supporters.

They will call you a clown, a fool, and a joke. But in the process they are the ones who end up looking like clowns; they are the ones making fools out of themselves; and they are the ones turning into one big fat joke.

The irony of satire is that anyone who takes it too seriously automatically turns into the very clown they think they are fighting against.

So why do we have to go through this? Will a revolution ever work? That might be a bit more difficult than we thought. For one very good reason: money.

DO REVOLUTIONS REALLY WORK?

FROM TAHRIR TO OCCUPY WALL STREET: A BULLSHIT ANALYSIS

You had your own version of a little revolution when a bunch of young adults did a Tahrir-style sit-in at Wall Street. For a country that touts its freedoms and right to assembly, how did that go? Free speech in America is a lovely thing but can it alone change the monopoly of the banks and the corruption of big business and their strong lobbies in Congress?

Many are starting to recognize that American democracy is actually changing into an oligarchy. People are vocal about all the imperfections of the system and yet free speech alone might not even leave a dent in the problem, let alone fix it. When people get more physical, they get crushed by the militarization of their own police. That's why the Occupy movement was looked upon as a bunch of crazy hippies who wanted to disrupt the system. Well, isn't a revolution, by definition, disruption of the system?

You might ask, *What does this have to do with the Egyptian Revolution?*

Well, there are actually quite a few similarities. The revolution came to disrupt many interests. After sixty years of military rule, soldiers get too relaxed and found other battles to fight. Like the ultimate battle to fill their bank accounts. In Egypt over the past few decades the army became more of a private corporation. The details of their budget are kept secret. They control a huge chunk of the economy, including the monopolization of many industries. Considering they don't pay taxes, customs, utilities, transportation costs, and even no decent salaries, since the soldiers are forcibly drafted and work as slaves in their factories, there is a huge amount of money filling their coffers.

The army in Egypt owns everything. They own the land, they own the resources, and they own the power to destroy your business if they want.

Over the past few years they went into all kinds of businesses, from construction to retail to mining. Nothing was off limits to the money-hungry generals.

They even have their own hotels, bakeries, and beauty centers. It is not uncommon to see a sign reading THE ARMED FORCES WELCOME YOU! SPECIAL RATES TODAY ON BRAZILIAN WAXING!

In 2016 the army announced the opening of its first ever private international middle and high school. The headmistress of the school said in an interview that although the school adopts the American educational system, she still believes that an American conspiracy is targeting Egypt. "There is a fortune teller in America whose prophecies all come true. He predicted that in one of the Arab countries [Egypt], there will be a president who pretends to represent Islam [Morsi], though he is far from it. And that the president who comes next would unite the Arab region and destroy the American economy. That president will have a name made up of two repeated syllables—he means SISI."

When I openly talked about the army's economy on Facebook, all hell broke loose. Every single media outlet was out there to get me. There was even a television poll asking people if I should be put on military trial for treason and executed. Well, that's a comforting thought. I was a threat to them even when I was in exile and not active in Arab media.

The military didn't mind having the Islamists come to power. As a matter of fact, the Muslim Brotherhood during their "honeymoon" period with the military were after anyone who remotely criticized the military. They were the perfect conservative and religious shield for the military's interests. It was only when the Brotherhood wanted a bigger piece of the pie that the generals got pissed.

A revolution is not just about freedom of speech, but the ability to monitor authority and hold it accountable. When a revolution fails, whether in Tahrir Square or Wall Street, it's always because someone doesn't want to get caught. It is imperative that they keep their privilege of milking the goods of the country any way possible.

You have a more "chic" way of affecting the outcome of elections and rigging political control. You have lobbies, complex interest groups, gerrymandering, and Citizens United.

For us, that convoluted system is too costly, so we use religion, fake patriotism, and plain brutal force and oppression. We have no time to hypnotize people with sports, sex, and entertainment. And our leaders are too proud to give a margin of freedom so people can blow off steam and criticize them. When I think of the military junta that controls the country now I don't think of them as generals or army officers who just want absolute power. I think of them as a bunch of businessmen in military uniform who will protect their economic interests with tanks and machine guns. As with most any corporate or government fiasco—follow the money trail and you'll find the greedy turd sandwich causing all the problems.

Of course there are other reasons for failing revolutions and why dictatorship is a chronic disease in the Middle East. There are social, religious, sectarian, historical, and political reasons for that.

But this is not that kind of book. For deeper and more accurate analyses go get one of those boring books published by Washington think tanks or political science departments in fancy Ivy League universities.

I don't have the credentials or even the desire to be that deep!!!

Now let's finish this goddamn book and try to leave you with a word of wisdom or something!

THE MIDDLE EAST DOES NOT HAVE NINE LIVES

Just when I thought I'd left the madness behind me, I came to America to find the Orange Menace taking over your country. *Is it me? Am I bringing bad luck everywhere I go? Am I a dictator magnet?*

My wife was sitting next to me as we watched Trump win. She looked at me with this incriminating stare, as if she was asking me, *Is this what you brought me to?*

Right between us was Nadia, our four-year-old daughter, sleeping and totally unaware of all that mess.

I looked at her and wondered if her beautiful brown skin and her curly black hair will cause her any trouble in this new country.

Did I move her from a country that would attempt to crush her will, independence, and free thought to a country that would judge her as an outsider, as an alien, as a threat?

So, America, I hope you do something about that Trump. Consider this book a warning for what is yet to come. Honestly, I am running out of places to go, and Canada is too fucking cold.

I couldn't help but look back at the past five years, the turmoil I have gone through, and ask myself, was it really worth it?

The scene might look disturbing and the whole "Arab Spring"

concept might look like it was a failure, a step backward, and an unnecessary disaster, but I don't think I have any regrets. I have had an incredible journey. I went from being a heart surgeon to being the host of the most popular show in the region's history. Our little one-hour weekly show exposed a whole system that was founded on fear and brutal force. I am flattered to see religious figures who were considered holy go after me. I feel tickled that military leaders were shaken to their core over a few cleverly written jokes. I managed to "get under the skin" of a baseless authority, even if it was just for a little while. In a society that is programmed to say "yes, master" I bucked the system and firmly said no. And I said it with a smirk and a wink and a nod—and that pissed the hell out of them. I did that hoping that my daughter will also follow suit. She will not be told what to do. She will grow up and if she chooses to say no it will be said without fear of being reprimanded or judged for it.

I might not be strong enough to continue to tell jokes against my oppressors right now, but maybe we were not meant to see the result or the victory that we hoped for. Maybe it was for another generation, for our children . . . for my daughter.

I see how my work inspired millions of young people around the Middle East to make their own contributions. With every video, vine, and meme, I see the youth using the Internet to challenge the hideous propaganda machine. They are finding ways to make fun of these brutal dictatorships, and in a small way I feel that my show is still going on. A revolution is not just an event, it is a long process. And the process might start with those young people losing respect for the establishments that controlled and brainwashed their parents through religion and fake nationalism. Those young people are questioning everything. Nothing is off limits and nothing is taboo anymore. Questioning in itself is a prequel to a revolution. The fall of the social, religious, and military idols that controlled the Middle

East is already happening. Those idols are losing their most important asset, being respected and being revered. The young generation is not taking this bullshit again. They may rule for a while with fear and brutality but the respect is long gone. It is just a matter of time.

But again, I am no political analyst, no global thinker, and no credible source of information. And I don't have to be any of those things to recognize that the Middle East still looks pretty messy. So now that I have some distance from my experience there and can put things into perspective, I can't help but wonder: Was there ever any chance for the revolution to succeed? I mean, I still think it was worth it, but was there any hope at all?

And I found that the best way I can answer this question is through physics.

If you are familiar with quantum physics you might have heard of Schrödinger's cat. This is a thought experiment in which a cat is placed in a metal box with a radioactive material and a capsule of poisonous gas. If the radioactive material decays, this will lead to the release of lethal gas that will kill the cat. But until you open the box, your knowledge of the cat's fate is inconclusive. It could be dead, alive, or some other outcome your consciousness has yet to perceive. You won't know until you open the box. This experiment opens the door to the idea of multiple universes with endless possibilities and scenarios. A universe with a live cat and a universe with a dead cat.

In our case, we could have had multiple scenarios, depending on power shifts and the intended or unintended consequences of each action. There could have been a multitude of universes with unlimited outcomes different from the one we are living in now. But I can firmly state that in all the possible outcomes for our universe, the one remaining constant is that the Arab world will always be fucked!

ACKNOWLEDGMENTS

No one reads acknowledgments, but since you got this far you might as well know who contributed to this heinous piece of work and total waste of trees.

I have to start by thanking Robert Guinsler from Sterling Lord Literistic, who duped me into writing a book in my second language. I don't know if he really believed in my story or just wanted to get his cut as a book agent. But, dude, the joke is on you, and this horrible book is now on your conscience forever.

I would like to thank HarperCollins for picking up this book to publish. For the life of me I don't know why a prestigious establishment like you guys would risk their reputation for this. At HarperCollins I had the privilege of meeting real people. Yes, believe it or not they don't have automated phone service. They have real human beings who actually guided me and who had to endure my horrible English and lack of creativity to produce this book. If you think the book is bad, you should have seen the earlier drafts. I was told that many quit their jobs at Harper, quit the book industry, and gave up on life when they had to review the book. Matthew Daddona, for a year you guided and edited this book. Thank you for your patience. Jeanie Lee and Karen Richardson, I don't know who you are but I guess you were the last two copy editors standing who tried to make sense of what I wrote. I can only imagine how you were suffering while editing this book, as you witnessed your mother language being murdered over nearly three hundred pages by a Middle Easterner like me. Now *that*, my friends, is real terrorism. Thank you very much.

I wanted to thank Lara Thomas Ducey, a beautiful soul and human being who really helped to transform this book from a collection of primary school–level writings into something that could be almost passable for adult-age readers. Thank you for being patient and accommodating and above all for being an amazing friend.

I didn't realize that getting original photos and obtaining permissions and licenses would be that hard. My friend Doaa Sultan from Egypt tracked down every photographer to get that out of their cold, dead hands. Thank you for all your lovely work.

Dear beautiful reader, I appreciate you being part of my journey within the pages of this book. It was a bittersweet experience for me to relive some of those events again. Thank you, my friend. I hope you didn't regret paying for the damn thing, or that you can find a way to claim a tax deduction come April.

ABOUT THE AUTHOR

Bassem Youssef, dubbed the "Jon Stewart of Egypt," was the host of the popular television show *Albernameg*, which was the first political satire show in the Middle East. Originally presented as five-minute videos on YouTube, *Albernameg* grew to become the most watched television program across the region, with 30 million viewers tuning in every week. It received wide acclaim around the world, with coverage on some of the biggest media outlets, topping off with Youssef's appearances on *The Daily Show* with Jon Stewart in June 2012 and April 2013. In June 2013, Youssef hosted Jon Stewart on *Albernameg* in Cairo, marking the second season's peak.

Some of Youssef's accolades include being named one of *Time* magazine's most influential people of 2013, being recognized by *Foreign Policy* magazine as a leading global thinker of 2013, and being awarded the International Press Freedom Award by the Committee to Protect Journalists that same year.

Youssef's most recent project is *Democracy Handbook*, a ten-part series exploring topics of democracy on Fusion.net. Youssef was also a visiting scholar at the Center of Democracy, Development and the Rule of Law (CDDRL), Stanford University, and continues to give talks around the United States.

Youssef majored in cardiothoracic surgery, passed the United States Medical License Exam (USMLE), and is a member of the Royal College of Surgeons (RCS).

Printed in the USA
CPSIA information can be obtained
at www.ICGtesting.com
LVHW031131310824
789807LV00005B/151